Once in a while, you come across great advice and wonder why you didn't receive it earlier in your life. This book is full of such advice. And like all great advice, the content of this book has stood the test of time and will remain as true for the current generation and the generations to come as it was for the generations gone by.

To classify this as a personal finance book would be to limit its potential. It is a great guide on how to live life itself and reiterates the things which are important in life. I am sure this book would be of great benefit to anyone who reads this with open mind, and then uses it to simplify their life and personal finance but this is of special importance to the salaried class.

My only regret while going through this book was the fact that I was reading it ten years too late. However, as the old saying goes, 'better late than never'.

—Anurag Singh
Vice President
JP Morgan Chase & Co

MASTER YOUR
MONEY
MASTER YOUR
LIFE

ABHISHEK KUMAR

First published 2019
Reprinted 2020, 2021, 2022

Disclaimer: The ideas, concepts and the principles discussed in this book are author's opinion on the subject matter it covers and is designed to provide information that the author believes to be accurate based on his research and experience. The publication is sold with the understanding that neither the author nor the publisher is offering individualised advice tailored to any specific portfolio or to any individual's particular needs. If legal advice or other expert assistance is required, the service of a competent professional should be sought.

While the author and the publisher have used their best efforts in preparing this book, they make no representations or warranties with respect to the accuracy or completeness of the information contained herein, and both the author and the publisher specifically disclaim any responsibility for any liability, loss, or risk, personal or otherwise, which might be incurred as a consequence, directly or indirectly of the use and application of any of the contents of this book.

ISBN 978-81-8328-530-8

Published by
Wisdom Tree
4779/23, Ansari Road
Darya Ganj, New Delhi-110 002
Ph.: 011-23247966/67/68
wisdomtreebooks@gmail.com

Printed in India

For your wealth
For your prosperity
For your happiness
For your success and
For your freedom
I dedicate this book to you.

Contents

Apply Fertilisers

Protect the Tree and Relish the Fruits

Foreword

This is an astonishing book. Abhishek has an uncanny knack for taking very complex financial issues and reducing them to prose that is easily accessible to a wide cross-section of people. There is something in this book for everyone, from the layperson to the finance professional. The advice given in this book will change your life for the better. Among other things, it will teach you about the tactics used by financial advisors, how optimal investment strategies can avoid succumbing to marketing gimmicks and the benefits of compartmentalising spending to ensure a secure financial future. I have always felt that professional finance education focuses too much on paradigms that are largely irrelevant for the general public. A book that makes finance accessible to laypersons was sorely needed. Abhishek's praiseworthy effort capably fills this void, and I wish him all success. The book has the potential to change many lives for the better and I hope it becomes a standard reference in many households across the country. I thank Abhishek for this invaluable effort.

—Avanidhar Subrahmanyam

Acknowledgments

This book would not have been possible had my wife Rakshmi not stood by my side all through its making. Penning down this book has been a long, stressful and finally a rewarding journey for me. The emotional roller coaster had me at times happy, at times sad, at times full of anxiety and at times empty; looking at the future without getting a clue on what lay ahead. Rakshmi not only endured it all but also kept me sane and focused and encouraged me to continue writing, in times good and bad. I wish I could have put her name as the co-author of the book. Maybe we can work together as co-authors soon where she would also write some part of the book in addition to bearing the different moods of the writer within me!

To my friend Pulkit Srivastava who did the difficult task of reviewing the first draft of the book and giving me the necessary feedback and suggestions to make the book more useful for the readers. Not to forget my father-in-law, Janak Raj Bhatia for providing invaluable suggestions to improve the content of the book. It was his long experience of handling and managing money which prompted me to refine parts of the book which focused on 'debt' to make them more practical. And many thanks to my father, Anil Kumar for inculcating the wisdom of financial discipline in me right from my early days. Many of the principles that you would read in the book are those of my father camouflaged in my words.

A very special thanks to Prof Avanidhar Subrahmanyam for the lovely foreword he has written to the book. To have earned the praise of a man of Prof Subrahmanyam's calibre and accomplishments is one of the best rewards I can boast of.

I would also take this opportunity to thank the esteemed professors and practitioners who took out time from their busy schedules to review the book and added value to it by providing their encouraging endorsements. Ram Kumar Kakani, Vivek Rajvanshi, P Venkatesh, Ramana Sonti, Satyabrata Jit, Sirish Gouda, Suman Saurabh, Shrinidhi Prahalad and Anurag Singh; I am deeply grateful to all of you for all your wonderful words.

Finally, I would like to thank my publisher and editors at Wisdom Tree for bringing out the book in the present form. A special mention to Shobit Arya as it was his constant guidance and nudge which made the finished product far better than what was initially presented to him. It was his encouragement, persistence and faith in the value and need of the book which pushed me to cross the finishing line. Thank you Shobit for bringing out the best in me. I learned a lot working with you.

—Abhishek Kumar

How It All Started

The day was 19 March 2011. I remember this date vividly because on this day I had received my Post Graduate Diploma in Management from the Indian Institute of Management Kozhikode. After a gruelling first year and a fun-filled second year, the time had come to say goodbye to my alma mater and enter the corporate world.

With an Engineering degree from IIT BHU, Varanasi and an MBA from IIM Kozhikode and having made my parents proud of my over-hyped branded degrees, I thought I was all ready to take on the world. With such a pedigree, a job in the Corporate Banking Division of a leading bank and a deep desire to succeed, I thought I would be rising up the corporate ladder quickly and very soon I would be making money in the leagues of Jordan Belfort (*The Wolf of Wall Street*). Oh boy! How wrong was I!

After a brief hiatus of two months at home and a formal training of banking for around three months at my company's corporate office, I joined the regional team of my division in Bengaluru. The team was small; rather, I would call it very small for an organisation which had around 40,000 employees on its payroll. I was the third member of the team and we had to look after the credit requirement of all the large corporate clients of the whole of south India.

Very soon the year had passed and it was the time of appraisal, bonus and hike. I was told that management trainees (campus recruits) usually got the default, which meant that they would not be judged but be given an 'Average'. I was no exception and I too was assigned the 'Average' rating. When I discussed it with my boss, he said that since I had been in the department only for six months, I had to be given an average rating as they didn't have sufficient data to judge my performance. I told him that it made all the more sense to appraise me better as I had done the same amount of work which a normal experienced person does in a year. He didn't listen and I had to buy the idea that probably it was the bank's policy to assign the default appraisal to campus recruits and there was no point discussing it further.

The following year I worked hard. I mean really hard. I used to go early and stay late working on deals, both existing and new. I thought probably the management would take notice of my work and acknowledge it with a better appraisal, better bonus and a better hike. This extra effort was more of my personal desire to get approval and appreciation from the senior management as this was what I assumed would help me leapfrog in my career. But again, the result was the same, 'Average'. This time I was crestfallen. I didn't understand what I should have done to succeed in my career.

Maybe hard work alone isn't enough, I thought to myself. This, for me, was a shocking realisation, raised as I was to believe that reward came to those who earned their living by the sweat of their brow. After consulting a few of my friends and colleagues, I understood that to go up in the corporate ladder, I had to be in the right place, do the right kind of work which would easily be recognised by the top management and I had to be in the good books of my boss and her immediate boss.

Now came the major challenge for me. Being located in the regional office in Bengaluru, all these things looked difficult, if not practically impossible, as all the heads of my department were based in Mumbai. I realised that if I wanted to progress in my career, I had to shift to Mumbai because that was where all the cream was, where all the big deals were signed. I also understood that it was not the case just with my bank; the practice was prevalent across all banks. Mumbai, being the financial capital, houses all the headquarters (HQs) of all major banks and financial institutions of the country and the decision makers of all these institutions were based there. So there was no point in switching my job to a different bank if I wanted to stay in Bengaluru.

Having stayed in Bengaluru for some time with my wife working in a technology company and seeing the fast-paced life of Mumbai, we decided that it didn't make much sense to move to Mumbai because as a family unit we would be at a loss both in terms of cash inflows and personal time we spent together. So, I decided to change my career—from banking to IT/ITeS/ Analytics—a major decision considering the fact that I wanted to build my career in the field of finance. With the best of degrees under my belt, I thought that getting a job would be a cakewalk. The market proved me wrong and I was again made to bite the dust.

After facing rejections from a number of companies; having exhausted almost all the opportunities that I could have possibly thought of and seeing no other possible way in which I could turn my career around, I was sinking into the dreadful zone of depression. I brought down the frequency of phone calls to my native town, started fearing about losing my job and took up the office calls apprehensively, thinking that somebody would scold me for the errors I presumed I had made. Many a time I used to ponder as to what mistake I had committed towards myself or others for which I was suffering in the manner I was. Going to office started becoming painfully difficult and though I tried to be sincere with my work while hiding my emotions and pain, the fear of job loss was becoming too heavy a load for me to carry. So one fine day I decided to hand over my resignation even though I didn't have any other job offer at that time.

The decision to resign was one of the turning points of my life. First of all, I felt a sense of relief that I did not have to be in the job which I had almost started hating. The happiness of being relieved from the job was something I had never felt in the previous two years of my professional life.

Second, I got the opportunity to interact with the regional head of my department at a personal level. What I learned from him in that one hour of discussion changed the way I perceived the job, money and life as a whole. He said, 'Abhishek, there are too many thorns all over the world. You have two options to make yourself safe. Either, you pick up a broom and start clearing the thorns or you put on a boot and walk safely. The choice is yours.' And what did I do? I chose to wear a boot. And since then I started working on myself, making myself stronger so that I could withstand any negative externalities that I might have to face in the future. I started developing my abilities which would help me sail through all the troughs and crests of life. I am thankful to him and express my heartfelt gratitude for imparting his knowledge and wisdom to me to live life more meaningfully.

Then one day good fortune came my way. Why did it appear at that moment in my life? Why do good things happen when they do? I really don't know. For me, this is part of the mystery of life. Anyway, my good fortune came when I went to a bookshop and my eyes fell on the book *Think and Grow Rich* by Napoleon Hill. I bought it, read it and then re-read it. And while I was reading the book, I imagined Napoleon Hill sitting beside me and talking to me about the wisdom he had learned from 500 of the most accomplished and successful people of the world of his era, from Henry Ford to Theodore Roosevelt to Thomas Edison to the richest and the most powerful person on the planet of his time—Andrew Carnegie.

The book was an eye-opener for me. It introduced me to the concept of money, wealth and prosperity and made me realise that by changing my attitude and outlook, I could guide my life in whichever direction I wanted to. I also understood how by channelling our energy, wishes and desires we could get whatever we wanted in life. I learned that all these successful people focused relentlessly on their goals and combined their desire, faith and persistence to achieve their ambitions. And I got to know something very beautiful—that I did not have to depend fully on my job to make my life prosper, that there were multiple ways in which I could create and increase my wealth and that the monthly salary was just one of the means to increase my net worth. *Think and Grow Rich* is one gem of a book and I don't recommend you to only read it; I suggest you devour it. Make it a part of you and your way of life and you will definitely thank me for that.

Having grasped this life-changing wisdom in a short span of thirty days, I had two options to move forward. The first was to work really diligently at my job, then articulate my accomplishments to my colleagues, my boss and my friends at my bank's HQ so that my work got noticed by the management, and keep my boss always happy and project myself as an over-enthusiastic employee who was always there to take care of the interest of the bank and its clients in the hope of a better reward from the organisation. The second was to be sincere at my work, expect nothing great from the organisation and at the same time start managing my finances and exploring different ways to increase my wealth.

I chose the second option. Why did I do so? Because by then I had realised that I could get more when I expected more from myself rather than expecting it from others.

For the next three years, I went on a quest to find out how money really worked, how I could get control of it and how I could develop the confidence to handle it. I decided to learn lessons that were not taught in a typical college finance class. I devoured every book I found on personal finance, wealth management and behavioural finance. I began to learn about money, its characteristics and the mistakes that normal middle-class people make which doesn't enable them to move into the elite group of the rich and successful people. Besides that, I came to know about the various myths about money and wealth which have become popular in our present culture and which are being practised by even the most literate and educated masses.

This quest then led me to a really, really uncomfortable place—my mirror. It made me realise that my money problems, worries and shortages largely began and ended with the person whose reflection I saw in my mirror, that was, myself. Also I realised that if I could learn to manage the character reflected in the mirror, I could win at money.

And then, I started following those principles I had learnt during my quest, kept myself away from the money myths—which I have discussed extensively in this book and incorporated the ideas of the great people into my life—and…I prospered. In fact, I started creating and accumulating money which wouldn't have been possible even if I had been the blue-eyed boy of my boss.

But the most gratifying experience of my journey was when I shared those ideas with my office colleagues, friends and relatives.

However, when I started discussing the ideas with these people, I realised that most of us don't have the skills to help ourselves because of the way we have been brought up and taught that being selfish is one of the greatest sins you can ever commit. To me being and doing good to yourself is not a crime; it is a virtue because until and unless you help yourself, you will not be able to help others. Remember, an empty jug cannot quench the thirst of people.

My first book *The Richest Engineer* was the result of my knowledge acquired in those difficult years and my desire to spread that knowledge about money and its rules to the people at large. The book was a 'wake-up' call to all the dormant souls who wanted to make it big in their life but were not confident enough about how to proceed. The book gave them the hope to win and that caused them to take action and claim victory over their financial struggles and worries, and to actually win. The emails I have been receiving from the readers across the country is just a testimonial that *The Richest Engineer* has played a small but important role in turning their lives around and giving them a definite direction in which they can sail their boat of financial freedom.

My present book is yet another attempt to bring back the old wisdom which seems to have been lost in the present-day busy life. The knowledge and wisdom shared in this book is not mine but that of all the great people—authors, scholars, professors—who have spent a considerable part of their lives collecting and integrating this knowledge which can be used by anyone to uplift his/her life. I cannot claim that all the content written in this book is entirely mine. I have learned the subject from some of the finest finance professors of the world. Also, I have learned from many excellent books such as *Your Money or Your Life* by Vicki Robin, *A Random Walk Down the Wall Street* by Burton Malkiel,

The Total Money Makeover by Dave Ramsey, *Millionaire Next Door* by Thomas Stanley and William Danko, *Money: Master the Game* by Tony Robbins, *The Four Pillars of Investing* by William Bernstein, *The Little Book of Common Sense Investing* by John Bogle and, of course, *Think and Grow Rich* by Napoleon Hill. In fact, these books have had a profound impact on me, and my explanations are influenced greatly by these books. If there are some similarities between my work and those by the great authors as mentioned above, it is due to the fact that I could not make any improvements upon the original explanations. I am very thankful to the authors for writing these great masterpieces.

I have also stolen some of the wisdom from our parents and grandparents and tried to repackage that experience and knowledge in a way which will not only answer the need of the present generation but prepare them for their future and that of their next generation. I repeat, I claim little or almost no originality in any of the wisdom and principles discussed in this book. However, with the knowledge and wisdom I have acquired over the past few years, coupled with my own experience in executing this knowledge and seeing its results in my life, I simply offer a new presentation of these ideas in a format people can relate with and implement in their life easily.

Now, as you read the book, let me help you with its structure. Imagine you are planting a tree so that you can relish its fruits when it grows and bears them on its branches. Just like there is a well-defined process of planting and growing a tree, there is a clearly determined process of wealth creation too. You cannot hope to get the sapling break the crust of the soil just by watering it if you haven't planted the seed in the first place and you can't expect to increase the yield of your tree just by adding fertilisers if you haven't taken steps to kill the pest which might destroy the roots of your tree. Similarly, when it comes to wealth creation you just can't have your net worth be increased by some solid investment if you haven't knocked off your debt or haven't put a working financial plan in place. And you can't achieve your desired prosperity if you haven't aligned your thought process and attitude towards money, both of which are conducive to the wealth creation process. Accordingly, the book has been divided into five parts where each part is a prerequisite to succeed and advance onto the next stage. Do pay attention to each part and try to extract the essence from it because it will be those fundamentals which will add as the nectar you carry to your next level of prosperity.

PLANT THE SEED

Chapter 1

Unleash the Power of Goals

Working as a corporate banker has its own perks. You get opportunities to meet the CEOs, CFOs and CXOs of leading corporates of India Inc. at a relatively young age. And after few meetings and conversations, you develop a rapport with them. I was indeed very lucky to have developed such a relationship with the CFO of a leading company based out of Bengaluru. He was over fifty years old but had the charm, energy and enthusiasm rarely seen in the present generation, even those who are in their thirties. He lived in one of the city's suburbs and had two kids, both of whom were pursuing their higher education in the USA. For our present discussion, we will call him Mr Anand.

One day, after the meeting, we were having a cup of coffee and some snacks when I asked him how he had become so successful and how he had managed to create so much wealth.

He didn't answer me immediately. After he had finished his cup of coffee and the office boy had cleared the table, he put down his specs, relaxed a little by stretching himself in his chair and said, 'Abhishek, tell me about your list of goals. Which are the goals you would want to accomplish in the near future, say in a couple of years and which are the goals you have visualised for the next ten years?'

'I don't have a list with me,' I replied.

'Well, then it must be on your laptop, mobile phone or written somewhere in a diary.'

'Sorry Sir. But I don't have such a list with me anywhere,' I replied ashamed.

Mr Anand sighed. 'Well, looks like today you're going to get your first lesson of wealth building.'

He looked directly into my eyes and said, 'I am sure that you being a banker would be earning a handsome salary. But, since you don't have a list of your goals, I can guess your bank balance would be in lakhs, if not in thousands.'

He had hit the nail on the head. And this really had me hooked. I was surprised. 'You mean to say if I had a list of goals, my bank balance would have multiplied?' I asked.

'Drastically,' he said smiling.

That day I became a student of the art of goal setting.

Of all the things I have learnt during my early days, goal setting has had the most profound effect upon my life. I realised how setting a goal, preparing a plan to accomplish it and then working towards achieving it could change one's life for the better.

After I understood the importance of goal setting and had chalked out my strategy to achieve it, I started working towards it. Meanwhile, I thought of asking my colleagues about their goals. Was I the only one who didn't have any goals or were there many who were in the same boat? One day, I asked a senior colleague of mine in the office about his goals. He had over fifteen years of professional experience and was one of the senior-most colleagues in our department. He looked at me slightly perplexed. When I repeated my question, he said, 'As such, I don't have any specific goals as of now.'

'Then why are you working so hard in the office? I have noticed that you are always the first one to come and many a times you stay late,' I asked.

'It is because I have to look after my family, pay my home loan EMI (equated monthly instalment), utility bills and tuition fees for my kids,' he said with a grim face.

'If that is your main purpose of working so hard in the office, why don't you move back to your native town? Then you wouldn't have to pay your home loan EMI. Further, your utility bills, tuition fees for your kids and other expenses would be substantially lower. And considering that presently you spend nearly two hours commuting daily in the Bengaluru traffic, you would be able to spend more time with your family as you would be wasting less time in the traffic.'

He was taken aback by my reasoning.

This is not the story of any one particular person. This is seen across all levels of employees and in all industries. Most of the people working in the corporate sector are sincere, hardworking and have an above-average IQ. Everybody wants to be successful, rise high up in the corporate ladder and accumulate wealth for their family. Yet, not everyone is able to become rich and successful. And the primary reason for their failure is not lack of intelligence, sincerity or commitment. They fail because they have never taken out time to prioritise their life and list specific goals for themselves. They fail because they let their talent and potential remain unutilised, thinking that is the maximum they can do. And they fail because they think lack of time is their major problem when lack of direction is, in reality, the main problem. JC Penny expressed it beautifully when he said, 'Give me a stock clerk with a goal and I will give you a man who will make history. Give me a man without a goal and I will give you a stock clerk.'

Correlation Between Goal Setting and Wealth Creation

Mark McCormack in his bestselling book, *What They Don't Teach You at Harvard Business School,* tells of a Harvard study conducted between 1979 and 1989.[1] In 1979, the graduating students of the MBA programme at Harvard were asked, 'Have you set clear, written goals for your future and made plans to accomplish them?'

It so turned out that only 3 per cent of the graduating students had written down their goals and plans for their future. Another 13 per cent had goals, but they had not penned them down. They had set goals for themselves which were floating somewhere in their minds. And 84 per cent had no specific goals at all, besides passing out of the university, enjoying the summer and taking up a job.

Ten years later, in 1989, the researchers interviewed the members of that class again. They found that 13 per cent of the batch who had unwritten goals were earning, on average, twice as much as the 84 per cent of students who had not set any goals for themselves. But, most surprisingly, they found that the 3 per cent of graduates who had specific and unambiguous written goals when they passed out from Harvard were earning, on an average, ten times as much as the other 97 per cent of graduates in all. The 3 per cent students who had turned professional did not have much difference in their intelligence, sincerity or hard work as compared to the others. The only difference between the groups was the clarity of the goals they had set for themselves when they graduated.

I will now add another perspective to the mentioned research. If you have noticed, the research mentioned was conducted on the graduating students from Harvard University which is considered to be one of the best universities in the world. And students studying there are some of the brightest scholars from across the globe. So, if only 3 per cent of the brightest pool of students had written down their goals, then imagine what percentage of the general masses would have written goals for themselves. I guess it would be less than 1 per cent. And no wonder, the top 1 per cent of world's population have accumulated more wealth than the other 99 per cent combined.[2]

Goals Give Direction to Your Effort and Energy

We human beings have been gifted with an analytical brain which functions continuously. Until and unless we are in deep sleep, we keep thinking. Most often it is about ourselves and our future. And when it comes to thinking and planning our future, we generally have two options: To face the future with anticipation or with apprehension. Guess how many of us face the future with apprehension? Right! Most of us do.

We have seen people who are forever worrying. They worry about their promotion, their hike and their salaries. They worry about the approval from their boss and how their peers perceive them. They worry about their subordinates not completing the work on time. They worry about their health. They worry about the minor dent their car had in the morning. And most of the time, they worry about the performance of their kids in school. Why are these individuals so apprehensive about everything?

It is mainly because they haven't spent time designing and planning their future. Many of them live their lives by forever attempting to win the approval of someone. And who is this 'someone'? This 'someone' is mostly their colleague, their boss, neighbour and distant relative whom they don't like much. And these are the same people who don't focus on winning the approval of people who really matter—their friends and family. In the process, they end up 'buying into' someone else's perception of how life should be lived instead of living the life they could have chosen to live. They fight each day of their lives in the war zone of economic survival, choosing existence over substance. No wonder they are worried—always looking around, appeasing everyone but themselves and seeking approval for everything they do.

On the other hand, those who face the future with anticipation have planned a future worth getting excited about. They have listed their goals and work regularly towards accomplishing their ambitions. They visualise the future in their mind's eye, and it looks terrific!

Dr Thomas Stanley in his ground-breaking work, *The Millionaire Next Door*, talks about a wholesale food businessman who was a multimillionaire. This man had started his business at the age of nineteen. Though he never finished his formal high school education, he received his high school equivalency diploma at a later stage of his life. When he was asked about his success and how he, despite being a high school dropout, was able to accumulate over $ 10 million, he replied:

'I have always been goal-oriented. I have a clearly defined set of daily goals, weekly goals, monthly goals, annual goals and lifetime goals. I even have goals to go to the bathroom. I always tell our young executives that they must have goals.'

Once I was going from Bengaluru to Mumbai. When I took my boarding pass I didn't go to some random gate. I went to the gate from which I could board my flight to Mumbai. And once I got off the plane, I didn't catch the first cab and tell the driver, 'Why don't we just drive around for a while because I don't know where I have to go'. Instead I told him the name of the hotel and the road where it was located. And once I reached the hotel I didn't walk randomly into any room. I took the key of the room I had been allocated and headed straight towards it. The point is that we don't wander aimlessly around when it comes to such a simple and plain thing as a trip, but we seem to think that aimless wandering will work with our life and our money. Remember, people who win at anything and everything have written goals. Goals are what you aim at; they give direction to your life. Zig Ziglar, the renowned author and speaker said, 'If you aim at nothing, you will hit it every time.'

Working without a goal is like an illusion. You get the feeling that you are doing a lot of things, but they aren't what you want. You are just busy fulfilling everyone's dream except yours. Setting your goals gives you clarity on what you ultimately want. It makes you crystallise and articulate the desires floating in your mind. It ensures that you are channelling your time, energy and efforts into things that really matter to you. In essence, it makes you live more consciously. And I would say, that is a better way to live—living consciously.

I have seen many intelligent and brilliant people living a lukewarm life and existence just because they have surrendered to the goals their parents thought for them, or the society thought or, most importantly, their boss and organisation wanted them to achieve. If you think you deserve something better, then you need to break this monotony and create a life of your own. Zig Ziglar once said, 'I don't care how much power, brilliance or energy you have, but if you don't harness it and focus it on a specific target, you're never going to accomplish as much as your ability warrants.' The lion that captures a wild beast doesn't go out and start attacking the herd, he selects one beast as a specific target and drags it home.

Without any reservation, I say that no matter whosoever you are, wherever you are and whatever you do, you should have goals. As Brian Tracy has rightly said, 'A person of average intelligence with clear goals will circle around a genius who is not sure what he or she really wants.' Students should have goals. Sales people should have goals. Housewives, mothers, doctors, bankers, engineers and athletes should have goals. You must have a goal because it's just as difficult to reach a destination you don't have in mind, as it is to come back from a place you've never been to.

Have Enough Reasons

After Mr Anand explained the importance of setting goals and penning them down, he gave me another piece of advice. He said, 'Most people have a low bank balance because they don't have enough reasons to accomplish their goals.' And then he added, 'People fail not because they are not intelligent enough, but because they don't have enough reasons.'

And that was my second lesson on that day: Have enough reasons to accomplish your goals.

Do you have enough reasons to accomplish your goals? If not, then I would suggest that you better think about and visualise the reasons for the goals you aim to achieve. Why do you want to achieve your goal? For whom do you want to accomplish it? What purpose will it serve? Do you have something to prove? Who will benefit by your achievement? Will it bring happiness to you and your family?

As you can see, there could be almost as many reasons for people to do well and accomplish their goals as there are people. The key is to have enough reasons and formulate them.

I have found out repeatedly that 'goal' is like your destination, but 'reason' is your driving force; it is the fuel which will propel you to reach your goal. A goal without a reason is like a body without a soul. If your goal is to become the vice president (VP) of your organisation but you don't have enough reasons to accomplish it, then chances are that you may not be able to reach that level and in case you do become the VP, you would have spent considerable time on your journey. However, if you could visualise the happy and smiling faces of your family members, a bigger bank balance, higher respect from your colleagues, friends and relatives and improved self-esteem, all of which you would attain once you became the VP, then the chances of your becoming a VP in a relatively shorter period of time would increase manifold.

Remember, if you have enough reasons, then in all likelihood, you will be able to accomplish your goal.

Why Don't People Set Goals?

If goal setting is so important, then why don't people have clear goals for themselves? Well, there could be multiple reasons for it. However, the most important of them all is that most of the people believe that they already have goals and hence do not need to set something new until they have achieved those goals. Seems logical but there is a catch here.

What most people consider to be their goals are not really goals but mere fantasies. After discussing with many people and enquiring about their goals, I have found that most of the people define their goals to be:

- 'I want to become rich.'
- 'I want to be happy and contented.'
- 'I want to lose weight.'
- 'I want to become successful.'
- 'I want to attain a very high post in my organisation.'
- 'I want to become a good father/mother and take better care of my kids.'

And the most famous and generic goal is: 'I want to do something big in my life.' You may be smiling while reading this, but it is nothing less than day dreaming.

Let me state it clearly. These are not goals at all. They are mere fantasies that are common to everyone. A goal, however, is something distinctly different from a wish. It is clear, written and specific. It can be quickly and easily described to another person. You can measure it and you know when you have achieved it or not.

Peter Drucker in his article *Management by Objectives* says that goals have to be SMART. What he really meant was that a goal should be Specific, Measurable, Achievable, Realistic and Time-bound.

In the table given below, we will see how we can decide whether we harbour a fantasy or we have set a goal for ourselves.

Fantasies	Goals
I want to become rich.	I need to increase my net worth by ₹1 crore in the next seven years.
I want to lose weight.	I need to lose 10 kg in the next six months.
I want to attain a very high post in my organisation.	I need to become vice president/director/partner of my organisation in the next five years.
I want to become a good father/mother and take better care of my kids.	I will spend a minimum of two hours every day with my son/daughter and will play with him/her every weekend.

One of the key characteristics of a goal is that it needs to be time-bound. If there is no time limit set for the goal then you will keep on procrastinating and chances are that you may not be able to achieve it. However, by setting a time limit, you push yourself, you start taking actions and then you put yourself on the path which will ultimately lead you to your goal. Diana Scharf has said it correctly, 'Goals are dreams with deadlines.' I would add another element to it. I would say that goals are dreams with a deadline and an action plan.

The second reason why people don't set goals is that they have never been taught to set a goal for themselves. When we were children, it was our parents who decided what our goals should be. We were always told how many marks we should target at in our school and board exam, we were told which colleges we should aim to seek admission in and in most of the cases we were told what kind of partner we should choose to marry. And, it didn't end there. Even after marriage, our parents set goals for us; for instance, by what age we should have kids and how many kids we should have.

So here is a guy who is twenty-five years old, ready to enter the corporate world but has never set goals for himself. It comes as no surprise to me that when he joins the workforce and starts earning, it is not him but his boss and organisation who will decide the goals for him.

Once I was attending a review-meet of my company in an upmarket resort. The top management of the company gave a presentation on what had been our achievement during that particular year and what we should target at so that we could register a 20 per cent growth in our bottom line.

I looked around the people attending the meeting. All of them were seasoned bankers, sincere and hard-working employees. And they nodded in agreement with whatever the top brass was telling them to do. I knew they would not let down their top management. They would leave no stone unturned so that the company was able to clock a 20 per cent growth the following year. Here I witnessed how the organisation had set the goals for its employees so that it could grow and increase its shareholder value. All organisations know and understand that they can grow and increase their valuation only when they set goals for themselves and lay down an action plan for their employees.

But what happens to the goals of the people on their personal front? Who cares? As long as the employees feel that they are doing something and the share price of the company for which they are working is increasing, everybody is happy. But my question is whether all the employees are really happy increasing the share price of their respective companies. I have my doubts.

I am not saying that you should not work towards achieving the goals of your organisation. But before you do that, you should set your own goals. You should prioritise your own life before working towards making the shareholders' lives better.

There is a simple way, which is to align your goals with that of your organisation. When you set your goals which are in alignment with those of your organisation, then both of you will grow. For example, if you set a goal of earning a sales commission of ₹3 lakh in the current year and your organisation has set a target for you to achieve a sales turnover of ₹50 lakh, then both your goal as well that of your organisation are in tandem and both have a good chance to grow together.

Activity is Not Accomplishment

Many of us believe that when we are busy doing something we are achieving something. Well, that may not always be the case.

Noted French naturalist and botanist, Jean-Henri Fabre once conducted an experiment on pine-processionary caterpillars.[3] These caterpillars have a special characteristic. They instinctively follow the silken trail of the caterpillars preceding them.

One day, Fabre took a flower pot and placed a number of pine-processionary caterpillars in single file around the circumference of the pot's rim. Each caterpillar's head touched the tail of the caterpillar in front of it. Fabre then placed the caterpillars' favourite food, the pine needle, in the centre of the circle created by the caterpillars' procession around the rim of the flowerpot.

Each caterpillar followed the one ahead of him thinking that it was heading for the food. Those tiny insects went round and round in circles for seven days! After a week of this mindless activity, the caterpillars started to drop dead because of exhaustion and starvation.

All that the caterpillars had to do to avoid death was to stop the senseless circling of the flower pot and head directly towards the food which was placed less than six inches away from those ever-circling crawlers. However, the processionary caterpillars were locked into their set lifestyle and couldn't extricate themselves from the mindless behaviour because they had confused activity with accomplishment.

We human beings are different. God has given us the capability to choose our goal and change our direction so that we can accomplish it. But do we?

Many people commit the same mistake as that of the caterpillars, and as a result, they reap only a small fraction of the harvest that life has to offer. Despite the fact that untold and unlimited wealth lies within reach, they acquire very little of it because they blindly follow the crowd to nowhere. They follow the same methods and procedures for no other reason than, 'It's always been done that way.'

In this respect, they are as bad as 'this-old-boy down home'. His wife sent him to the store to buy ham. After he bought it, she asked him why he didn't have the butcher cut off the ends of the ham. 'This-old-boy' asked his wife why she wanted the end cut off. She replied that her mother had always done it that way and that was reason enough for her. Since the wife's mother was visiting them, they asked her why she always cut off the end of the ham. She replied that this was the way her mother did it; mother, daughter and 'this-old-boy' then decided to call the grandmother and solve this three-generation mystery. The grandmother promptly replied that she cut the end of the ham off because her roaster was too small to cook it in one piece. Now grandma had a reason for her actions, what about you?[4]

Setting Up Goals

Having understood the importance of setting goals and how setting our goals and penning them down helps us achieve our dreams, let us understand how we can set goals for ourselves.

Jim Rohn, the famous American entrepreneur, author and speaker has devised a unique way of setting goals. Goals need to be diagnosed and dissected in a detailed manner. And the best way to do so is to dissect them on a piece of paper with the help of a pen or a pencil.

I would like you to take out a paper and a pen and draw the table as given below. Now start filling it with all the possible thoughts that come to your mind. But before you do so, let me explain what these fields are.

Goal	Time to Accomplish	Detailed Description of the Goal	Reason for Achieving the Goal

Goal: It is your destination. It could be what you want to become, any material possession you wish to acquire, any specific amount of money that you want to accumulate or any specific experience that you want to realise, such as going on a vacation/trip.

As we discussed earlier, your goals should be specific, measurable and challenging. They must cause you to stretch a little bit and must be beyond anything that you have accomplished in the past. Also, your goals should have a minimum 50 per cent probability of success. This would make the process of striving towards the goal slightly stressful, but it would force you to stretch, bringing out many of your best qualities that you were unaware of.

Time to Accomplish: It is the number of months or years you believe it will take you to achieve or acquire each item on your goal list. Once you are done with this, you need to check if your goals are in balance. For example, if you find that you have too many ten-year goals but very few one-year goals, this could mean that you're putting off having to act in the present by postponing the target date. On the other hand, if you have very few long-term goals, perhaps you haven't decided what kind of life you want to build over the long run. The key here is to develop a balance between short-term goals and long-term goals.

Detailed Description of the Goal: Describe your goal in a detailed manner. For example, if you want to accumulate a certain amount of money then write it in both words and figures; if it is a material object, describe how long, how high, how much, which colour, which model and so on. On the other hand, if it's a position or a business that you want to start, give a detailed job description including salary, title, budget under your control, the number of employees and so on.

Reason: It is the most important of all. It is the soul of your goal. Here you need to put why you want to achieve or acquire the items described. Here, you'll find out whether you truly want it or if it's just a passing fancy. If you can't come up with a clear and convincing reason why you want it, you should categorise this item as a whim, not as a true goal and wipe it off your list.

You see, what you want is a powerful motivator and only a good reason provides that impetus. At times, you may find that some goal which you once considered important no longer has any appeal simply because you are unable to find a good reason for wanting it. That's good. This assignment will help you to reflect, refine and revise. And that's the crux of the matter—to help you plan your future.

Accomplishing Your Goals

When you are done with setting your goals and writing them down on a paper, it's easy to become overwhelmed by the process. My advice to you is, relax.

If you don't feel you're equipped to get what you want, remember Jim Rohn's words, 'Your ability will grow to match your dreams.' This is the magic of goal setting. As you start working on your goals, you'll draw on your untapped potential and talents that you never knew you possessed. And as time goes on, you'll draw from new reserves deep within your creative mind. Before you know it, you'll be able to accomplish things that seemed impossible to achieve.

Also, the more you work on your goals, more and more new opportunities will present themselves to you. You will start filtering out the thoughts and external factors which are not congruent with your desired goal and this will help you grab even more opportunities. And inside each new opportunity will be the seed of a solution to what previously appeared as an insolvable problem.

Brian Tracy, the world renowned speaker and author has said it very beautifully, 'When you are absolutely clear about your goal, you do not even have to know how to achieve it. By simply deciding exactly what you want, you will begin to move unerringly towards your goal, and your goal will start to move unerringly towards you. At exactly the right time and in exactly the right place, you and your goal will meet.'

So be fearless and get started. The journey will take you far beyond your wildest imagination. All you need to do is to value your goals, have faith in your abilities, buckle up and take the plunge into the sea. And once you do it, you will not be the same person again.

Why are goals so powerful? How can they cause all this to happen? I don't know. I guess this question falls into that special category I call 'mysteries of life'. All I can tell you is that it works because I have personally experienced it. Find out for yourself. Give yourself the chance to become all you can become and to accomplish all you are capable of.

Why a Chapter on Goals in a Book of Personal Finance?

You may be wondering why I have dedicated an entire chapter on goals, their importance and how we can set and accomplish our goals in a book meant to discuss money, wealth and personal finance.

It is because of my firm belief that no matter what I share or what you read, nothing will help you in getting what you want and put you on the path to success until and unless you have set a goal for yourself towards becoming rich and living the life of your dreams. Setting your goals and penning them down will inspire you to achieve them. Also, you need to have a proper reason to become rich and be financially secure and happy. It is this reason that will drive you towards your goal. Remember, defining your goals and writing them down is the first step which will drastically change your bank balance.

Endnotes

1. Harvard Business School Goal Story, http://www.lifemastering.com/en/harvard_school.html
2. As per the report published by International Committee of the Fourth International (ICFI) dated 14 October 2015, https://www.wsws.org/en/articles/2015/10/14/weal-o14.html
3. Lethal Fuzz, http://www.naturalhistorymag.com/features/21756/lethal-fuzz?page=2
4. 'Old boy down home': *See You At Top*, Zig Ziglar (1975).

Chapter 2

Understanding Money and Personal Finance

The education system in our country, or, for that matter, anywhere in the world, is designed to make people skilful and provide them with worldly knowledge and wisdom which they can use to make money or for any other occupation they wish to pursue once they graduate. However, it doesn't teach people certain soft skills, such as the art of dealing with people, setting goals and achieving them, managing money, forming habits which are conducive to being productive at the work place, etc. and which help them succeed in their chosen profession and lead a meaningful and fruitful life.

Why is it so? It is because all these skills are very personal and cannot be measured objectively. There are no crystal clear right or wrong answers. It will be extremely difficult for any education system to evaluate its students on such subjects. And if such subjects were taught where there was no evaluation and no grading methodology, hardly any students would choose to opt for them. It is better they are removed from the curriculum. Another reason why these subjects are not taught formally at the school and college level is because to appreciate them and benefit from them, the students need to experience them personally in their real life.

It is for these reasons that we have a bunch of high school students who graduate with elementary ideas of science, history and maths but have no idea how to operate a savings account or open a fixed deposit. Although they are taught about percentages, simple interest and compound interest, they are unable to apply the knowledge acquired in their real life when they choose not to invest their money early on in their career. And once the work pressure increases as they progress in their career, they become more focused on solving their company's and client's problems, forgetting the underlying motive for which they were working and their ignorance regarding the subject of money continues.

This ignorance about money and how to handle it properly is not something which has been continuing since time immemorial. Our ancestors knew and understood it much better than what we, the present generation, can claim to know. Chanakya, the famous teacher, philosopher, economist and royal advisor to the throne of the Maurya Empire had authored a literary masterpiece—*Arthashastra*. This treatise talked about the principles of law, economics and governance and was a complete guiding principle for the ministers, scholars and the masses until it was lost in the twelfth century. It was, however, rediscovered in 1904 by R Shamasastry and published in 1909. But by this time it had lost the importance that it had enjoyed by the masses during the second century BC and, subsequent to its rediscovery, its study is restricted to that by scholars and economists.

Ignorance is Not Lack of Intelligence; It is Lack of Awareness

Over a century has gone by and still a very large proportion of Indian citizens are ignorant of what money is and how it should be handled. Whenever I tell someone that one of the reasons that they are not rich is that they don't have knowledge of what money is, they get offended. They equate ignorance to lack of intelligence and then start defending themselves. The reality is that ignorance is not lack of intelligence; it is a lack of knowledge about a particular subject. For example, if I were placed in the Research and Development (R&D) centre of a pharma company, I would probably blow up something. But this doesn't mean I am unintelligent. It simply means that I am ignorant of the process of developing drugs. If you were required to undergo some surgery I doubt you would call me, not because I am unintelligent but because of my ignorance of medicine and the surgical procedure.

No one is born with the knowledge of how to read and write or how to drive a car; over the years we are taught these skills. No one is born with the knowledge and skills of making money; we are taught how to do so. And, no one is born with the knowledge of how to spend and handle money, but we aren't taught that. We go to school to learn how to earn; we earn and then have no idea what to do with our money. As mentioned earlier, no school or university teaches the basics of managing money and that is the reason why a major portion of the population, even the so-called highly qualified professionals, struggle with their money.

Suppose a person starts his career at the age of twenty-five with a starting salary of ₹3 lakh per annum, a very conservative figure to begin with. Let us assume that he gets an average hike of 10 per cent every year, taking into account the usual raise, promotion and job switchover during his working age, that is, till the age of sixty. During the working period of thirty-five years, this person—the average boy living next door—earns nearly ₹9 crore over his lifetime (without taking investing and compounding interest into account; this ₹9 crore is purely his salary income). Since he has never been taught how to handle and manage money; he struggles all his life, getting frustrated with his job and boss, the continuous stress of low bank balance, the ubiquitous monthly EMI to be paid, and ends up a dejected person. Now imagine what an individual who is financially literate and understands money, personal finance and how human behaviour and psychology affects our wealth creation and accumulation would do with this money of ₹9 crore.

Once again I repeat that if you have been struggling with your money and finances, it is not because you are not intelligent. It is mainly because you have never been taught how to manage and handle your hard-earned money. Worse, you have been taught all the wrong things about money by your bankers, brokers, credit card companies, jewellers and real estate developers. As author Josh Billings has said, 'It's not what we don't know that prevents us from succeeding; it's what we know that just isn't so that is our greatest obstacle.' And this book is not only about learning and overcoming ignorance, it is also about unlearning some predetermined beliefs and obsolete knowledge which are creating obstacles to your financial success.

Overcoming ignorance is easy. First of all, with no shame, admit that you are not a financial expert[1] because you were never taught the skill of managing your wealth. Second, read this book. Third, go on a lifetime quest to learn more of money. And for that, you don't need to enrol in some Indian Institute of Management (IIM) or Harvard or Oxford for a specialised course in finance and you don't need to watch the financial channel advising you to sell and buy stocks. But you do need to read something about money. There are many books and magazines on personal finance management available in the market. You need to discuss money and wealth with your spouse, colleagues and friends and, most importantly, with people who have and are accumulating more money than you. Your action should show that you care about money by learning something about it.

One of the good things that I have learned from reading the works of great men such as Napoleon Hill, Jim Rohn, Zig Ziglar and Brian Tracy is that if you wish to be successful, study success; if you wish to be happy, study happiness; and if you want to make money, study the acquisition of wealth. Those who achieve success, happiness and wealth don't do it accidentally. It's a matter of studying first and practising second. But not many people attempt to follow these practices as part of their studies. And that is one of the reasons why despite everyone wanting to become wealthy, they don't.

To say ignorance is bliss is wrong. Ignorance is neither blissful nor okay as far as money is concerned. Tony Robbins, who is a well-known speaker and life coach has said, 'Ignorance is pain, ignorance is struggle and ignorance is giving your fortune away to someone who hasn't earned it.' When it comes to money, what you don't know can make you stressed and may force you to go broke. So keep reading and learn more about money and personal finance and this acquired knowledge will help you accumulate so much wealth which you would have never imagined or dreamt of.

Understanding the Basic Characteristics of Money

In my discussion with people, I have realised that their problem was simply a lack of knowledge and discipline. Money has four properties or characteristics which most people don't acknowledge or understand and this creates some obstruction at their subconscious level in their path to financial prosperity.

Let us spend some time to understand what those characteristics of money are and how we can set our subconscious mind so that there are no unnecessary roadblocks in our journey to freedom.

Money is Active

Do you remember the size of a one rupee coin or a five rupee coin ten years ago? Now compare those with the present-day coins of the same denomination. You would have noticed that their sizes have shrunk considerably. What does it signify? It is just an indicative step by the Reserve Bank of India (RBI) to make the masses aware that the present ₹5 coin would purchase them less food than they were able to purchase with the same ₹5 coin ten years earlier. Well, there are people who would say that the cost of minting a ₹1 coin was higher than the value of the coin itself and hence to reduce the material cost they have reduced the size. Whatever may be the reason, the fact is that size of the coins has reduced in both the figurative and economic sense.

For the literate masses, the size of the coin doesn't matter. They look for value. They also understand that the value of money decreases with time. In fact, we all know that the value of money has been decreasing continuously because of inflation and it will continue to do so as long as there are inflationary tendencies. Yet, very few of us protect our money from inflation; we let our money depreciate with time.

You should understand that money in this sense is very active. Depending on various macroeconomic factors, it keeps on changing its value. Finance and money are always moving. Time, interest rates, inflation etc. intermingle to create an ever-flowing current. No wonder we also use the term currency for money which has been derived from a Latin word 'currens' meaning 'to run or flow'. Like a river, money must keep flowing; otherwise, it begins to clog and stagnate. Circulation keeps it alive and vital. And to keep it alive and vital we need to keep circulating the money by manipulating its flow. The better we are at manipulating it, the more of it we will control.

Think of money as an untamed beast which has a mind of its own. To gain control of this beast and to enjoy its ride you must control it, otherwise very soon you will fall down. Similarly, if you want to take control of your life then you should exercise control over your money or otherwise it will control your life forever.

Remember, if you don't continually take action on your money, it, or the lack of it, will act on you. Finance is not passive. It requires you to take the initiative to control it. In his bestselling book, *The Seven Habits of Highly Effective People*, Dr Stephen Covey says that the number-one habit of highly effective people is that they are proactive. They 'happen' to things; things don't 'happen' to them.

Money is Amoral

Most of us attach a sense of morality to money and generally the society is divided into two groups in this respect. A particular section of people thinks that lack of money will make them immoral, that is, it will force them to commit immoral activities in order to survive. However, there is another set of people who believes that too much money will force them into immoral indulgences.

What most people don't understand is that money in itself is neither moral nor immoral. It is amoral. Dave Ramsey, a noted author and speaker on personal finance says, 'Just because you are poor doesn't make you good or spiritually superior; neither does it mean that you are bad or spiritually inferior. On the other hand, having wealth doesn't mean that you are inherently good, nor does it mean that you are a crook and have accumulated wealth by unfair means.' You decide what you are. The way you act through your money or your lack of it will show whether you are good or evil, but money is neither of the two.

Money, in this sense, is like water. It takes the shape and inherits the qualities of its possessor. Remember, money is nothing but an amplifier. It amplifies the internal habits of its possessor. The same money in the hands of a teacher can be used to buy books for students and in the possession of a terrorist is used to buy guns to kill the same set of students. It is not money which decides to what use it should be put to; rather it is the possessor of the money who decides its usage.

Money is a Measure of Your Inner Self

Imagine our life to be a tree. The fruits that the tree bears are nothing but our successes, accomplishments and failures. Depending on the quality of the seed and how it is planted in the soil, and how the tree is nourished by way of providing water, manure and fertilisers, the tree bears the fruit.

Very often when we look at the fruits, we don't like them. There aren't many of them, and in most of the cases the fruits are either too small or their quality is below our expectations. So what do we do? We start focusing on improving the quality of fruits by watering the tree and sprinkling it with pesticides. And what happens with our increased effort? It is the same quality of fruit but with our increased effort the number of these not-so-good fruits (failures) has increased and we feel depressed and dejected.

In our attempt to improve the quality of fruits, what we often forget is that it is not the water, pesticides or fertilisers which create the fruit. It is the seed which has been planted in the soil and the resultant roots of the tree which create the fruits. Water and other materials just help in the process; they don't create the process.

We should understand that it's what is under the ground that creates what's above the ground. It's the invisible that creates what's visible. And what does it mean for us in real life? It just means that if you want to change the fruit, you will have to change the roots. If you want to change the visible, you must first change the invisible.

Rich people know this and that is the reason they focus a lot on changing and improving what is 'under' the ground. And what is this stuff which is under the ground? It is your belief, your thought process, your habit, your knowledge, your wisdom and your overall personality. And how do you improve the 'internal stuff'? It is by constantly improving yourself by way of seeking, reading, learning and doing things which are conducive to wealth creation.

Harv Eker, the famous American author says, 'Your income can grow only to the extent that you do.' Rich people know that their income will never exceed them. They understand that the amount of money that they make is just a reflection of what is inside them. And that is why they focus a lot on improving themselves. They read a lot to acquire knowledge. They keep themselves updated in their respective domain to remain competitive in this fast-changing world. They also gain knowledge and wisdom on how to create and accumulate wealth. They improve their network by meeting new people and gain valuable insights from them. In simpler terms, they follow the rule that to have more money than what you've got today, you've to become more than what you're today.

Physicists agree that nothing in this world is static. Everything alive is constantly changing; even our earth and universe is changing. Take a simple example of a plant. If a plant isn't growing, it is dying. It's the same with the people as well as with any other organisms; if you are not growing, you are dying.

Remember, physical wealth may be a piece of paper or some number in your bank account, but true wealth is an intrinsic value that starts with you. When you focus on yourself and possess the billionaire mindset, the wealth will follow. The only way it gets better for you is when you get better. As Jim Rohn has said, 'Better is not something you wish; it's something you become.'

People often ask how one can earn an above-average income. The answer is very simple. It is by becoming an above-average person. Income rarely exceeds personal development.[2] Sometimes income takes a lucky jump, but unless you learn to handle the responsibilities that come with it, you will ultimately have only the amount you can handle. A very rich man once said, 'If you took all the money in the world and divided it equally among everybody, it would soon be back in the same pockets it was before.' It's hard to keep that which has not been obtained through personal development.

The fact is that your character, your thought process and your beliefs are a critical part of what determines the level of your success. Stuart Wilde, an American author, puts it this way: 'The key to success is to raise your own energy; when you do, people will naturally be attracted to you. And when they show up, bill them!'

Money is Also a Reflection of Your Contribution to the World

In my study of the rich and successful people, I found one thing in common among them—they have contributed a lot more to the society than the average person. Think of Ratan Tata, Dhirubhai Ambani, Azim Premji or Narayana Murthy and you will realise how much they have contributed to the society in terms of providing job opportunities, economic empowerment of the public and the country at large and general welfare of the society through their corporate social responsibility (CSR) initiatives. Even if you consider celebrities like Shahrukh Khan, Sachin Tendulkar or MS Dhoni who are among the elite club of 'Rich India', you will see they have contributed a lot in terms of entertaining the masses and playing and bringing laurels for the country.

Rich people know and understand that wealth is nothing but a by-product or a reward for their contribution and/or service to the society. And that is why they don't exactly focus on generating wealth directly. Rather, their focus is on increasing and improving their contribution to the society and the state at large. Bill Gates became rich not because he wanted to become the richest person on the globe but because he wanted to see a computer, which could be easily operated in each and every household. Steve Jobs became rich not by running after money or doing some odd jobs just to make his living. He became rich because of his desire to bring the services and applications of the computer/laptop which people could access even when they were 'mobile'. Remember, your salary or influence is not an end in itself, but a measure of your contribution to the world.[3] As Tony Robbins has said, 'The secret to wealth is simple: Find a way to do more for others than anyone else does. Become more valuable. Do more. Give more. Be more. Serve more. And you will have the opportunity to earn more.'

There is a universal law which is unknown to most people. It is called the *Law of Giving and Receiving*[4] which is based on the fact that everything in the universe operates through dynamic exchange. This law is simple: If you want love, learn to give love; if you want attention and appreciation, learn to give attention and appreciation; if you want material affluence, help others to become materially affluent; and if you want to be blessed with all the good things in life, learn to silently bless everyone with all the good things in life. The more you give, the more you will receive.

Rich people know this law and that is the reason that their main focus is on making lives of other people better. They know this simple fact that in your willingness to give that which you seek, you get to keep the abundance of the universe circulating in your life. No wonder most of the philanthropists in our country and the world are the rich and successful people. And the notion that you need to be rich to give and become a philanthropist is wrong. Rather, the truth is when you start giving—be it material substance, service or simply your wishes and blessings—is when you receive and you start becoming rich. Remember that when you start giving even at the times when you think you have very little, you'll teach your brain to think that there is more than enough for you. And with this, you leave the 'poor mindset', the 'scarcity thoughts' behind and move towards a world of abundance.

Understanding Personal Finance

Having understood the basic characteristics of money, let us spend some time in understanding what exactly personal finance is. As there are a number of misconceptions among the masses about this subject, it is imperative that we spend some time in understanding this subject which has been so much misunderstood and misinterpreted.

Personal Finance is More Than Just Investment, Insurance and Taxation

Whenever I say 'Personal Finance' the very first thought people have is of investments, stock market, mutual funds, taxation and retirement planning. And they talk about it with as much disinterest as if they are being forced to drink some bitter-tasting herbal syrup.

You should understand that personal finance is not only about investment, insurance, Sensex, taxation and retirement planning. It is about how you manage your money. It is about setting priorities in life and allocating your money accordingly. It is about setting goals and working towards accomplishing them. And it is about changing yourself so that when you are able to create and accumulate wealth, you will discover a newer and better version of yourself. As Jim Rohn has rightly said, 'The major value of reaching goals is not to acquire it, but it's the person you become while you're working to acquire it.'

Personal Finance is More of an Art and Less of a Science

Most of the people with whom I have discussed the subject of money and personal finance consider it to be a subject of mathematical science. Since there are numbers, percentages and formulas, they treat it as a subject of nerds and geeks. This is true in most of the cases because that is the way it has been taught to people in colleges and universities. And that is how our brokers, bankers and chartered accountants explain it to us. However, Dave Ramsey, the famous American author and speaker, has a different take on finance. He says, 'Finance is an exact mathematical science—until a human touches it.' Personal finance is who you are. The personal, philosophical and emotional strengths and weakness that you have will be reflected in the manner in which you use your money.

If personal finance was an exact mathematical science then all the average families with the same range of salaries would be equally rich or poor. However, that is not the case. The reality is that different people within the same set of salaries or income accumulate different levels of wealth because personal finance is more of personal and less of finance. And since different people have different levels of strengths and weaknesses, the levels of wealth they accumulate also differ. Larry Burkett, a noted author on this subject says that money problems are not the real problems but instead are only the symptoms of a personal shortfall.

So, how do we solve the real problem and not merely cure the symptoms? It is by understanding some of the myths that have been taught to us by various entities with vested interests. It is by learning some of the basic principles of money and laws of wealth creation. And most importantly, it is by being disciplined enough to cruise ahead.

Personal Finance is As Much About Spending Money As It is About Earning

People often confuse personal finance to be only about earning and investing money. Almost all the books, magazines and journals on personal finance will talk about investments, asset allocation and portfolio management. However, they overlook the fact that managing your money encompasses not only earning and investing but also how you spend your money.

The problem with people struggling with their money is that they think they don't know how to make a good amount of it. What they really don't know is how to use the money they already are making. After you reach a certain level of income generation, getting additional increment in your income will not help much. What will really help is how you manage that money by spending and investing it judiciously. Ironically, in our mad race to earn more and more to become rich as quickly as possible, we forget this important step of managing money and that is why most of the people are never able to come out of this vicious circle. Remember, if you are having trouble with your money then chances are that you may not have an income problem; what you might be having is the spending problem. But worry no more. This book will talk as much about how to spend money as it will discuss on earning and investing.

Personal Finance is 80 Per Cent Behaviour and 20 Per Cent Technical Knowledge[5]

Most people believe that to become really rich they need to have a very good and thorough understanding of all the technical aspects of finance and the financial industry. And since they are already occupied with their existing job and since they have so many other things to do, they usually give up the hope of understanding finance and with it their dream of becoming rich.

What people don't realise is that they don't need to be a financial expert to become rich. If technical knowledge was a prerequisite to becoming rich, then all the finance professors and bankers and the so-called finance experts who come on prime-time shows to advise you to buy and sell stocks would have been rich. But that is not the case. Technical knowledge of financial markets, investments and tools do play a part in helping you become rich but their contribution is much less than what is usually assumed. The major part comes through common sense and self-discipline and for that, you don't need to go through an advanced course in finance and accounting.

Personal Finance is Not Complicated; Rather It's Very Simple

What I have realised in my study on money and success is that some of the most profound and life-changing wisdom you will ever discover is very simple. But in our culture we have started praising and following the complicated and the sophisticated. We have started believing that an investment which is not sophisticated will not fetch us good returns. A lot many people I have met are of the view that simple ideas are not profound, that instead, simple ideas are meant for the 'novices'. They believe that if they want to make a good profit, they need to put money into some sophisticated instruments. After all, they are educated and smart. This is a completely false notion.

As a corporate banker, I had the opportunity to go through the financial statements of some of the richest people of corporate India. And after perusing those statements, I have realised that in almost every case these millionaires keep their investing and money philosophies very simple. They always keep their balance sheet simple and clean. Only the so-called financial experts, the agents and brokers like to complicate things for the sake of justifying their existence. These experts/brokers/agents know that they will not be able to bargain the quantum of fees and commission from you if they present things in a simple and lucid way.

The financial industry often works to make this topic feel incredibly complex but, in reality, once you get past the jargon, it's relatively simple. This book is your opportunity to stop being the chess piece and become the chess player in the game of money. I think you are going to be very surprised at how with an insider's understanding of the financial market which this book is going to present to you, you can easily transform your financial life and enjoy the freedom you deserve.

Personal Finance is Also About You and Your Habits

The last point which I would like to drive home in this chapter is to help you understand one simple but powerful concept. It is that to gain control over your personal finance, you must get better control of all aspects of your life. Until you do that, the lessons and knowledge that you get from this book will be of no use to you. If you're a shopaholic, then no matter what I teach you, you will end up messing up your finances until and unless you change yourself and get your priorities right. If you take drugs or drink and it affects your finances, then you should recognise it as a sign of addiction and must seek 'counselling' because I cannot help you overcome your problems at that level. No matter how much I talk about getting your finances in order, you will spend your last penny on booze and the entire effort of reading this book will go waste.

Human beings are creatures of habit. More often than not, you will be guided by your habit and emotions than by your brain.

Since getting rich is the result of your action and the action comes from your habits, you should learn to inculcate the habits of the rich people by observing and studying them. Remember, first you build the right habits and then those habits will build you. However, building right habits which are conducive to wealth creation is not an easy task but, once built, they are easy to live with. Wrong habits on the contrary are easy to acquire, but difficult to live with. Almost without exception, wrong habits come slowly and pleasantly and, in most instances, the habit takes hold of you and before you're aware of it you have become a slave of it.

Zig Ziglar said, 'When you choose a habit, you also choose the end result of that habit.' Rich people understand this and that is why they devote a major part of their life building right habits which are conducive to wealth creation and accumulation and then getting rich becomes automatic. Before picking an action they visualise what the end result of that particular action will be. Will it help them accumulate wealth or will it deplete them of their savings? Will that action bring additional income or will it add an unnecessary item on their expense list? And as they are able to see the end results of their actions, they choose those actions carefully keeping their emotions at bay for a while because it is those actions which once repeated will become their habit. Remember, habit is like a rope and we weave a thread of it each day until it becomes too strong to break. Then the strength of that habit 'rope' takes us to the top or ties us to the bottom, depending on whether it is the right habit conducive to wealth creation and accumulation or the wrong one.[6] As John Astor has said, 'Wealth is largely the result of habit.'

The following poem discusses beautifully how your habit can build or kill you and it is up to you how you want to use it. The author is unknown.

I am your constant companion.
I am your greatest helper or heaviest burden.
I will push you onward or drag you down to failure.
I am completely at your command.
Half of the things you do you might as well turn over to me
and I will do them, quickly and correctly.

I am easily managed; you must be firm with me.
Show me exactly how you want something done
and after a few lessons, I will do it automatically.
I am the servant of great people, and alas, of all failures as well.
Those who are great, I have made great.
Those who are failures, I have made failures.

I am not a machine though I work with the precision
of a machine plus the intelligence of a person.
You may run me for profit or run me for ruin, it makes no difference to me.
Take me, train me, be firm with me,
and I will place the world at your feet.
Be easy with me and I will destroy you.

Who am I? I am Habit.

Please spend some time after reading this chapter in personal reflection. Write down the resolutions—those involving major and minor changes—that you feel you must make. Then spend time in making those changes in yourself as you read the rest of the book and gain the valuable insights which will help you live the true life that you have always wanted to live.

Endnotes

1. There may be financial experts who would be reading this book to gain more insight and that is what most of the experts do—continuous reading and learning. But again their proportion is limited and I hope it increases in future.
2. *Seven Strategies of Wealth and Happiness*, Jim Rohn (2007).

3. https://qz.com/932799/bruce-lee-achieved-all-his-life-goals-by-32-by-committing-to-one-personality-trait/
4. *The Seven Spiritual Laws of Success,* Deepak Chopra (1994).
5. While this idea has been shared by many people, it has been made popular by Dave Ramsey through his books and seminars.
6. A popular phrase, the author is unknown.

Chapter 3

Determine the True Purpose of Money in Your Life

I often tell people that the most hardworking and the most sincere people in our society are the salaried middle class. They are the people who are ever ready to do their duty, be it rain, wind or sunshine. They will be in the office punctually even if there is a transport strike in the city or someone is sick at home. And these are the people who contribute a large percentage of personal income tax in India. But when it comes to living a fun-filled, meaningful and purposeful life they are right at the bottom of the pyramid.

Let us consider the life of an average employee in almost any metro or urban centre. The alarm rings at 6:30 am and our working man or woman is up and running—morning tea/coffee; shower; dress in the professional uniform; breakfast, if there is time, otherwise grab a bite of a sandwich along with a cup of tea or a glass of juice in the office cafeteria; grab the office bag including the lunch box. Then hop into the car or the bike for the daily punishment called the rush hour or on a bus or train packed crushingly tight; bear the mad traffic, deafening honking and pollution if driving or sweat of the co-passengers in the bus or a train; reach office and be on the job from nine-to-five. During the office hours, deal with the boss, the co-workers, other stakeholders and with the most important of them all, the clients/customers. He/She has to act busy, hide mistakes committed, smile when impossible deadlines have to be handled, give a sigh of relief when the axe, also known as 'restructuring' or 'downsizing' falls on other heads, thereafter shoulder the added workload with a lot of fake enthusiasm. Watch the clock. Argue with your conscience but agree with the boss. Smile again. Kids call. Tell them that papa/mama will be home soon. It's 6:00 pm now. But you need to wait longer to show to your peers and boss how dedicated and hardworking you are at the job; otherwise, how will you prove your dedication to the work during the next appraisal? Work if you have energy left or pass the time in gossiping or reading some online articles. Leave office at 7:30 pm; back in the car/bike and get stuck in the traffic or into the bus/train for the evening commute; reach home; act human with mate and kids; eat; watch TV; jump into bed. Eight hours of blessed oblivion.[1]

Do we call this making a living? Think about it for some time. How many people have you seen who are more alive at the end of the working day than what they were early morning? Do we come home from our so-called 'making a living' activity with more zest and enthusiasm for life? Do we enter through the main door refreshed with energy, ready for a great evening with the family? Where's all the 'life' we supposedly made at work?

For many of us, isn't it true that we are 'making a dying'? Aren't we killing ourselves—our health, our relationships, our sense of joy and wonder—for our jobs; our monthly pay cheque?

Vicki Robin in her bestselling book *Your Money or Your Life* says, 'We are sacrificing our lives for money, but it's happening so slowly that we barely notice it.'

Zig Ziglar, the famous American author and speaker, shared a story about how mediocrity sneaks upon us. The story goes that if you drop a frog into boiling water, he will sense the pain and immediately jump out. However, if you put a frog in room temperature water, he will swim around happily, and as you gradually turn the water up to the boiling point, he will not sense the change. The frog is lured to his death by the gradual change. The same is happening to us. We are slowly but steadily losing our health, our fitness, our relationships and our wealth, day by day. And the worst part is that we do not realise the loss of all that is valuable to us.

Are You Driven by Values or Stuff

One of the reasons why most people are not happy despite making and possessing a good amount of money is that they are not leading their life in harmony with their values. Now you may wonder what these 'values' are and how we live our life in alignment with them. Well, let me help you understand what exactly values are.

Values are those aspects of your life that matter most to you. Your value system, consisting of multiple values, gives you structure and purpose by helping you determine what is meaningful and important to you. This value system varies from person to person and that is the reason why different people seek and find happiness from not one but varied sources.

Still confused about what your value system could be? Well if I ask you to choose five words from the following list, then what you have chosen after deliberate and conscious thinking would be your value system—a system consisting of five values which you feel are really important to you.

Freedom, happiness, love, health, family, security, career, growth, fun, excitement, peace of mind, making a mark for yourself, fulfilment, power, marriage, friends, independence, spirituality, adventure, innovation, making a difference...

Your values are the guiding principles of your life and the driving factors behind your behaviour and every decision you make and execute. It affects how you communicate with your spouse, how you raise your kids and how you feel about what you have in your life. Your values determine how hard you are willing to work to achieve your financial goals, how much money you currently spend and how much money you feel you will actually need at retirement. With certainty I emphasise that once you have a clear picture of what you value most in your life, you'll be able to create a truly purposeful and meaningful life.

Noted author David Bach in his book *Smart Couples Finish Rich* has put this principle of values beautifully. He says that money is good for three basic things. 'It helps people...

'Let me help you understand what exactly these three terms are. When I say that money helps people "become", I mean that it allows them to live in a particular way that defines who they are. When I say that money helps people "do", I mean that it makes it possible for them to take actions that will help create the kind of lives they want. And when I say that money helps people "have", I mean that it enables them to buy the material things that they wish to possess.[2]

'Ideally, the lives we lead, the actions we take and the stuff we buy would always be in tandem with our values. The challenge is that most people focus first on the "having", second on "doing" and third on the "being", which essentially means that many people are going in the reverse gear. Worse than that is that many people never even get to the "being" part. They spend so much time in "having" stuff and "doing" things so that they can have more stuff that they forget who they are and who they want to be.'

In order to create a sensible and meaningful life, you must understand what money means to you and what values it can help you acquire. Once you know this, you can quickly focus your time and energy on what matters most to you—not what society, friends or advertisers and marketers say will matter to you, but what you feel and say will be important for you. To put it differently, the process is basically a matter of looking really deeply at what is most important to you and then planning your finances around that. Does it appear as if we're talking more about a life-planning process than just a money-management process? Well, quite frankly, that's what smart financial planning is really about—'values' first, 'stuff' second and then working your money around it.

Let's say you value 'security', but you are constantly spending more than what you are earning. As a result, you are living pay cheque to pay cheque. In other words, you are living your life which is in conflict with your value of 'security' and this will create a stress in your life. Why? It is because your financial behaviour simply doesn't match your personal concept of the value of 'security'.

Let's take another example. Suppose you value 'freedom', which to you means having time to go for a long walk with your spouse every day. Unfortunately, what you're actually doing is working sixty hours a week, which means you never get a chance to go for a walk or spend time with your spouse. Now you may be enjoying financial success—since you are working so much time at office and rising up the ranks—but how likely is it that you're happy? Not very, I assume. Why? It is because your professional behaviour simply doesn't match your personal value of freedom.

Or consider a common dilemma which most people encounter. Suppose you had 'family' as your top value. Now when buying a house, you purchased one which is big enough so that all family members—you and your spouse, your kids and your parents—have their own room so that all three generations can enjoy the benefit of staying together under the same roof. But you are so busy working in order to be able to meet your home loan EMI that you never actually see your spouse, kids and parents. You are in constant conflict with your value—you and your family are not together but separate; you in office and they in the big house. Someone talked you into buying a bigger home than you could afford, and now you are paying the real price. No one, including you, considered your personal value of 'family' when you purchased the house. Unfortunately, when you make major decisions like that without considering your values, what you end up with is stress and unhappiness. No one wins.

One of my friends once said to me, 'I watch my kids growing horizontally.' Well, what he really meant was that when he leaves for office early in the morning, his kids are sleeping and when he reaches home late in the evening his kids are in bed. And he is a soft spoken, family loving guy who made the mistake of purchasing a home beyond what he could afford so that he could give the best of the amenities to his family. Believe me, beyond a certain point, your kids don't care where they are staying and what they are driving. What they really care about is whether they are getting the love and affection of their parents or not.

Remember, money is great to have and it is equally great to buy stuff with that money, but all the money in the world won't make you happy if what you do with it conflicts with your values. To have a blissful life, all you need to do is decide what your top five values are, write them down and then start planning your life around them. The sooner you start putting your values first and stuff second, the sooner you will start living a life that excites and empowers you. That's because when you understand your values, you tend to live the life you really want almost automatically. Instead of having to 'motivate yourself' to do the right things, you find yourself being pulled in the right direction by the power of your values. Material things may be attractive, but they rarely take us anywhere worthwhile. Only values can do that.

How Wrong Ideas Have Been Sold to People

With the opening of the Indian economy, there has been tremendous growth of private businesses and the rise of the banking and financial sectors in particular. This has led to people being sold ideas and processes which they think are working for them. People have bought the idea of being financially well-off with material possessions—the stuffs. The more the stuffs you acquire, the better you become. Wrong! If these processes and ideas were actually working for them then probably they would not get themselves into the trap of living the life of a robot—waking up–rush hour–office–client–stay late–home–sleep–wake-up. Instead, they would be leading a life as per their wish and choose a profession as per their choice. What people don't realise is that these ideas and processes which they have been sold are not working for them but for the banks, credit card companies and other entities which have an active watch on people's pockets.

One of the tenets of the financial process and planning that has been sold to the public at large is the idea of borrowing. We have been taught continuously through various channels and mediums that we can purchase anything we desire without any money.

And how do we purchase those materials without our earned money? It is by borrowing. Banks and credit card companies have come up with an array of loans at our fingertips with which we can really purchase anything we want. And what is really scary is that people are actually purchasing things on credit. Right from a mobile phone to a washing machine to a car to a home; everything is being purchased on borrowed money. Someone has rightly said that the present generation has got this unusual ability to finance everything. Ask them if they would like to finance their vacation on an easy EMI and you would hear an instant 'yes' from them.

As a people, we have forgotten how to delay pleasure. We are living in a society that microwaves everything. We must have it and we must have it now. As Brian Tracy says, 'We are being taught by everything around us to have dessert before dinner.' Now we are paying for our lack of knowledge and discipline as we have got ourselves into the never-ending process of working in a job which we don't really enjoy but continue with, just to pay the bills and acquire material stuff to showcase how far we have come up in life. In reality and deep down in our heart we know this is not what we want, but we fight with our conscience and settle for it because that's how everybody wants us to be and that's how we have been taught to be. This is a typical instance where your actions don't match your values.

It's human nature to acquire materials and stuff and to enjoy the comfort and luxury that they provide. But we should learn to understand that acquisition of new materials and stuff will give us true pleasure only when they are in line with our values and when we purchase them with our own money. When you have huge EMI against your newly acquired car, you may not be able to really enjoy its drive. Although to the whole world you may appear to be progressing well since you have purchased yet another brand new car and you may also derive comfort in your ability to finance your car, somewhere deep down in your heart you are aware of the difficulty and effort with which you are managing your finances. While the world sees your car, it is only you who sees its EMI.

Is There Some Hope?

There is no denying the fact that we all want a good future for our family and especially for our kids. And so what we do? Well, usually we work harder or become a two-income family and sometimes depend on others to take care of our children. We earn for their college education, for their marriage but relinquish the opportunity to spend time with them during their formative years, substituting toys for time and a maid or a crèche for parents and family. We are spending so much of our precious time earning that we don't have the time to examine our priorities—our value system.

So how do we get out of this mess? How do we create a good future for our kids without compromising our life? How do we work and still take out time to attend our kid's programme in school without the guilt of bunking office? How do we live an authentic, productive and meaningful life and yet have all the material comforts we want or need? And how do we create and accumulate wealth for ourselves and our family?

The first step of coming out of this mess is to acknowledge that things are not going as per your wish. And how do you know if that is happening? The litmus test to answer this question is to check if the five values you have written down are being fulfilled. If they are not being fulfilled, then you must understand and acknowledge that things are not going as per your wish. This point of realisation that you are not financially fit and you need a makeover will solve a major part of your problem. Someone has rightly said that a major part of solving a problem is realising that there is one.

One of the problems with most people is that they live in a mode of denial and that is a major obstacle preventing them from winning the 'money game'. The typical salaried-class people are so busy in their job, in complaining about their bosses, peers and organisation and in continuously looking out for a greener pasture outside their organisation that they do not take out time to think about the real problem. In most of the cases, switching to another company doesn't solve the problem as it doesn't cure the real problem. It only changes the environment. The rules and structure that were present in the previous organisation are also present in the new set-up and very soon they get frustrated and either accept their fate or look for another so-called greener pasture and the cycle continues and frustration mounts.

To change your financial well-being, you must understand that you have to change. Changing your boss or your organisation will not solve the purpose. You need to change your view of the 'material stuff' and 'money' and you need to learn how to handle both so that your actions and possessions are in alignment with your values.

You must also understand that if you are not as wealthy as you want to be then the problem is not the lack of money or the smaller payslip that you think you are receiving. The problem is you. The news channel or some expert advice on prime-time shows isn't the answer; you are. As Dave Ramsey has said, 'If you're the one who got yourself into this (financial) mess, then you're the one who can get you out of it. No law, regulation or mandate will help you. No political party's promises or government handout will deal with your problem. No dream job or sky-high salary will secure you. Some of those things may help, but none of them will do anything unless you take charge of your own life.' This is your life, your call, your future. If you're ready to move, then let's get going!

Endnotes

1. A major part of this particular extract has been taken from the book *Your Money or Your Life*, Vicki Robin (Penguin USA).
2. This particular idea of 'Be-Do-Have' has been explained in detail by David Bach in his book *Smart Couples Finish Rich* (2001).

KILL THE PEST

Chapter 4

Debt: A Tool or a Propaganda

Once upon a time in a small town called Sonpur on the other side of the Ganga people of different professions and occupations lived in peace and harmony. While some people used to till their land and grow crops, others used their craftsmanship to provide goods and services to them and other people. There were a few who were also involved in trading and used to buy and sell goods and services from nearby villages. The primary medium of exchange of these goods and services were the metal coins that were being minted by the treasurer of the kingdom who ruled over the town.

As the economy prospered, the inhabitants of the town wanted to expand their business. But they had limited capital and hence they needed more coins. Also, there were people who needed coins to meet some of their personal needs. On the other hand, there were a number of people who had surplus coins with themselves and wanted to lend those coins to the people who needed them so that they could earn more coins. This market force of natural demand and supply led people with surplus coins to lend their coins to the people who required them and the process continued for some time.

Since there was no standard institution and platform, many a time people in need of coins were pawns in the hands of those who had surplus and the lender decided the terms and conditions of this lending–borrowing transaction. The chief of the town observed this and decided to set up an organisation which would accept coins from the people who had surplus and lend the coins to those who needed them. Thus an organisation was set up and named as 'People's Bank'. To run this bank, the chief employed people who would do all the paper work and work towards meeting the bank's objective—accepting coins from people and lending these coins to the people in need. And to meet its administrative expense the bank charged a little more interest from the people who borrowed and provided less interest to the people who lent their coins thereby, making its profit by way of a margin.

When the bank started working, its top management realised that actually the earnings of the bank came from lending, since people who borrowed from it had to return more money than what they had borrowed. Also, they realised that accepting coins from people was a liability for it as the money had to be returned after a period of time, with added interest.

So the top management thought of creating products—Debt Products—which they could sell to the people and start earning more. The objective with which the bank was set up—to provide a standard platform where people could deposit their surplus coins and people in need could borrow those coins—had changed. Seeing that it could earn while meeting its initial objective, the bank became an enterprise—a profit-making organisation—and very soon its main objective became to earn as much as possible.

And to meet its new objective the bank started selling its Debt Products to people.

One fine day, Vijay, a local trader who was passing by the bank overheard Thakur, the head of the bank, talking to his assistant, Mohan.

Thakur: So Mohan, you see we have been able to meet the public expectation. People are coming to us to deposit their coins and we have been able to lend those coins to people who need them.

Mohan: Yes Sir. It looks like we are doing a noble job. It makes me feel really happy.

Thakur: True. But, do you notice when we as a bank make money? Is it when we accept coins as a deposit from people or when we lend those coins?

Mohan: It is when we lend those coins. The borrower pays a lot more interest to us than what we pay to our depositor. It is as simple as that.

Thakur: Correct. Our borrowers are our actual customers, who work hard to return our money with added interest. And the more they borrow, the more money we make.

Mohan: But that is not our objective, Sir. We are here to provide a platform so that we can connect the lender and the borrower and these people do not have to spend time in looking for people to lend to or borrow from. Also with the establishment of the bank, the risks associated with individuals have been eliminated as we have been set up with the help of our village chief and people have more trust in us than in individuals.

Thakur: True. But in addition to meeting our stated objective, if we are able to earn and make more money, it is a win-win situation for us.

Mohan: But how we will make more money?

Thakur: It is when we encourage people to borrow more money from us. The more they borrow the more interest we will earn and the richer we will become.

Mohan: But how do we convince people to borrow more from us? These people are very sincere and noble. They live within their means. And borrowing is their last resort. They borrow only when nothing else works for them. Additionally, living on borrowed money is like a curse for them. They live with honour and making them borrow money without a genuine need will be very difficult.

Thakur: Who says there has to be a real need to borrow money? We will create an artificial need and glamourise it in such a way that people will come begging to us for money.

Mohan: Sorry, Sir, I don't understand.

Thakur: Have you noticed what borrowed money allows people to do?

Mohan: With borrowed money, people are able to purchase items which they can't afford to buy with their regular income.

Thakur: Correct. So don't you think we should encourage people to borrow more money?

Mohan: But there are so many problems associated with borrowing. First, with the borrowed money people will be inclined to spend more. Since they will spend money which they are yet to earn, there will be no emotional pain attached to it when they shell out the borrowed coins. Second, people have to return the money with added interest. So, in a majority of the cases the future income of these people will not benefit them but the bank which has lent them the money and they will not be able to improve their financial well-being. And, in all likelihood, these people will keep on working hard to bring income to the bank.

Thakur: Yes. And that is what we want. We want them to borrow money, spend it and work continuously to fetch us interest.

And that is how we will become rich sitting in this office and lending them money. It's the way people will become rich going forward. And we would be the pioneers. Lending money will make people rich and borrowing money will keep them poor.

Mohan: If borrowing money keeps people poor, why would they borrow? After all, many of the people who borrow from us are educated and would be smart enough not to borrow.

Thakur: Probably you don't understand human psychology. They want instant gratification. And with borrowing available at their disposal, they will be able to purchase things they desire immediately though it may not always be the most economical thing to do. And we are going to exploit this weakness. We will provide them with an array of loans so that they borrow more and more from us. We will provide them with a business loan, which is what we have been doing. Additionally, we will provide them with a housing loan, a loan for purchasing cattle, a loan for purchasing a cart, a loan for buying household items and groceries and a loan for general purpose. We will keep on adding different loan products to our portfolio. We will make them habitual of borrowing so that they keep on borrowing all throughout their life by buying one or the other loan products from our portfolio. And very soon with the interest earned from these borrowers we may not need deposits from the public to further lend them to the borrowers. We will have our own pool of coins and we would decrease the interest that we pay to our depositors as our dependency on them would have come down and this will increase our profit further. Mohan, my boy, I am sure we are going to become rich, very rich. We just need to make people borrow money from us.

After Vijay had heard and understood the conversation between Thakur and Mohan, he dropped his plan of going to another town to buy goods which he intended to purchase and instead went straight to Thakur and asked if there was some job opportunity in the bank.

The Time Has Changed but the System Continues

Now let us come to our present times and see how the prediction of Thakur, our bank chief, was on the dot. Thakur was definitely ahead of his times and he was right when he said that people want instant gratification. It is human nature to want it and want it immediately, without any delay, but it is a sign of immaturity as well. Being willing to delay pleasure for a better result is a sign of maturity and that is what we as sensible and responsible citizens should do. However, our culture teaches us to live for the now—'not in a spiritual but in a material sense'.

Take the famous Marshmallow Test,[1] a series of studies on delayed gratification in the late 1960s and early 1970s led by psychologist Walter Mischel, then a professor at Stanford University. In these studies, a child was offered a choice between one small reward provided immediately and two small rewards (that is, a larger reward) if they waited for a short period of approximately 15 minutes, during which the tester left the room and then returned. (The reward was sometimes a marshmallow, but often a cookie or a pretzel.) In the follow-up studies, the researchers found that children who were able to wait longer for the preferred rewards were healthier and more successful in their school years later on.

But in our present race of getting-it-now, we often forget about the benefits of the delayed pleasure and want instant gratification even if we don't have our own means to achieve that. 'I want that car and I can get it immediately. Yes, I need to get into debt for that. But I have a steady job and I can pay off the EMI. So let's buy a hatchback? No. Let's go for sedan or SUV. Yes, the EMI will be higher and we will have to stretch ourselves a little but we can manage it.'

Once I was having a discussion with my office colleagues during the lunch hour about purchasing a house. One colleague, who was actively looking for an apartment in Bengaluru, told me that he had found a good 2BHK apartment and would soon be making the down payment to book it. So I asked him how he was going to finance it. He replied that the price of the apartment was close to ₹90 lakh. He had saved ₹20 lakh and would be using it towards part payment and for the balance amount of ₹70 lakh, he would avail of a bank loan. Then I poked him and asked what if he had ₹90 lakh available with him. Would he still take a bank loan or make the payment fully on his own? To this he replied that if he had ₹90 lakh with him he would have no reason to go for a 2BHK. Rather, he would go for a 4BHK or a row house or even a villa in a posh locality, make the down payment of ₹90 lakh and avail of a bank loan to fund the balance amount.

The fact is that our present generation has been sold the idea of borrowing so that they can't imagine a life without debt, borrowings and credit card. We have been sold debt so repeatedly and with such fervour that most of the people cannot conceive what it would be like to have no monthly payments. Dave Ramsey, in his book, *The Total Money Makeover* says, 'Just as slaves born into slavery cannot visualise freedom, we, the present working generation, don't know what it would be like to wake up with no debt on our shoulders.' We have been bombarded continuously with advertisements and promotional mails and have begun to believe that debt is a way of life. As someone has rightly said that if you tell a lie often enough, loudly enough and long enough, the myth will become accepted as a fact.

Debt Makes You Feel Rich When You are Not

Earlier people used to take a loan for something like a home; then they started taking loan for cars and slowly they have graduated to taking loan for sofas, refrigerators and mobile phones. If you have been observant on the price tags the retailers put on furniture and electronic goods, you would have noticed that in addition to putting the retail price of the item, they also stick the EMI amount. They know that since people spend most of their salary, a bulk of which goes to pay the last month's credit card bill, they won't have any surplus to purchase a sofa of ₹50,000. So how do they sell their products? They can't wait for their customer to have a surplus of ₹50,000 at his disposal because the customer may never save that much amount to purchase a sofa. So what do they do? They provide their customer the 'not so' easy EMI option by allowing him to take a loan from their partner bank or non-banking finance company (NBFC) and off the customer goes with that sofa and yet another EMI to be paid over the next twelve months. And guess what? Most of the people are not buying those big-ticket purchases based on the actual price they would be paying but on the EMI they need to manage in their existing list of EMIs, and in doing so they pay in total nearly twice or thrice the amount of the actual price of the product.

Once when I logged into the online portal of a leading bank, I noticed some of the ads that were flashing on its colourful dashboard. The ads went something like this, 'Vijay bought his dream car. Do what he does. Choose our car loan.' Another one was: 'Deepika always shops her heart out. Do what she does. Choose our credit cards'. And the other was, 'Amit treated his parents to a foreign holiday. Do what he does. Choose our personal loans.' Never in those chain of flashing ads did I see something like 'Abhishek always invests ₹1.50 lakh in his Public Provident Fund (PPF) account right in the beginning of the year. Do what he does. Invest in PPF'. The question is: Why would they flash such ads? The bank is there to make money for itself and its shareholders and it can do it only by selling loans to people. Banks don't make that much money when you save and invest with them in the rightful tools, but they do make lots of money when you buy their loan products and spend your money.

Remember, banks don't only make money by earning interest on the loan that they just sold to you, they also get a cut from the retailers when you use their card or the internet portal to make payment to the retailers. So it's a double benefit for them. And yes, retailers too enjoy this set-up between banks and themselves as it becomes easier for them to sell goods without worrying about the purchasing power of the customer (as customers usually artificially boost-up their purchasing power by availing of a loan). No wonder banks spend so much money just to advertise how you will get a 5 per cent discount or some kind of cashback when you use their cards to purchase items from a particular store. I am yet to see an advertisement where I am offered an additional 1 per cent or even 0.5 per cent when I invest in some simple tools such PPF or purchase a term plan insurance from them.

Repetition Turns Myths and Lies into Truth

Repetition, volume and longevity will twist and turn a myth, or worse, a lie into a commonly accepted way of doing things. And that is what is happening in today's world. The entire population has been lulled into approving of ghastly deeds and even participating in them by gradually moving from the truth to a lie. Throughout history, twisted logic, rationalisation and incremental changes have allowed normally intelligent people to be party to ridiculous things. Propaganda and vested interest, in particular, have played a big part in allowing these things to happen. This propaganda is not of any government or political party but of certain groups of people who want us to think the way it serves their purpose and who will go to any length to accomplish that goal. The financial and banking sector, in particular, is very good at teaching us their way of handling money, which, of course, leads us to buy their products and services. Similarly, jewellers run their own propaganda and so do real estate developers and consumer product companies.

So why do these companies run such propaganda and what has all the propaganda led to?

The answer to the first question lies in the fact that all these companies, including banks and financial institutions are enterprises set up with the goal of making money for their shareholders. I am not saying that it is a bad or a sinister goal. In fact it's a noble goal and that is how every organisation runs and that is how our economy prospers. But when it comes to your money, you should be very particular about what is happening to it. You should understand that all these institutions are not set up for a social cause—to help people like you to make money—but they are set up to make a profit for themselves. They are not there to help you increase your wealth but to increase their own. And their main goal is not to help you realise your dream but to realise theirs. As Elliot Weissbluth, founder and CEO of High Tower, says:

> 'There's an inherent conflict in the financial service system. The largest financial institutions are set up to make a profit for themselves, not their clients. Investors may think that they are paying fees for high-quality, unbiased advice. Instead, they are all too often paying for the privilege of being offered a small sample of "suitable" investment products and services that are in constant conflict with improving the firm's bottom line.'

True, as part of their service, banks help people who are in real need, such as farmers or small businessman, but in reality, they don't like lending to them. They are forced to lend to them under the 'Priority Sector Lending' as mandated by the RBI at a much lower interest rate than what they normally charge from people in urban or semi-urban centres. But again, given a choice, no bank would like to lend to people who are in real need of money.

They will only lend to them from whom they expect to earn money. And who are those people? They are the typical salaried middle-class people. They are people like you and me.

You will never see any bank selling and advising young professionals who are joining the workforce to open a PPF account or go for a term insurance, which would be really beneficial for them in the long term, as banks don't make much money on them. But you will see all the banks selling credit cards when they come to open the salary account for these young men and women, as they know it is in lending that they make money.

So they offer credit cards and make it appear as if it is something exclusive when they tell them that it is being provided for free because these young men and women are joining the elite crowd of new age working professionals. In this way, they kill two birds with one stone. First, they sell their debt product—the credit card. Second, they make these young professionals get into the habit of using the card right from the first day of their pay cheque so that throughout their life these people would keep on working to make money for these banks and credit card companies.

Catch them young, make them loyal to your product, give them a feeling that they are part of an elite crowd holding that plastic and be relaxed. These people will earn, they will spend using the plastic and they will bring you interest income and commission (remember, cut from the retailers) while you sleep or catch yet another set of young people joining the workforce.

Now coming to the second question: What has such propaganda led to? They have created myths and have made lies turn into truths which have been accepted by the public at large. People have started believing in these myths and are taking actions which are in alignment with these myths thinking that it is normal and the smartest thing to do. And if you advise them anything against those myths, then be prepared for a long and heated debate.

Is It Wise to Gain Acceptance? Not Always

It is human tendency to be a part of group. When one stands out, he becomes an outlier and feels terrified that he won't be accepted into the group and that he would have to give a valid reason as to why he is not a part of the group. So he participates in what the crowd identifies as normal, even if it is stupid, and gains acceptance in the club.

We all have heard of the famous study done on monkeys to understand their herd mentality. If you haven't heard it, it's time to read about it and if you know it already, it's time to refresh your memory. It goes something like this: Some scientists locked a group of monkeys in a room with a ladder at the centre. And on top of the ladder some ripe bananas were placed. Whenever a monkey would begin to climb the ladder, the scientists would soak the rest of the monkeys with cold water. After a while, every time a monkey went up the ladder, the rest of them would pull him down and beat him up because they feared that they would be soaked in the cold water again. After sometime, no monkey dared to go up the ladder regardless of the temptation. Scientists then decided to replace one of the monkeys with a new one who didn't know the system. The first thing this new monkey did was to go up the ladder. Immediately the other monkeys beat him up. And after several beatings, this new member learned not to climb the ladder even though he never understood why. Now another monkey from the original group was replaced and the same thing occurred. Even the first new monkey participated in beating the second one. One by one, each monkey was replaced and the scene was repeated until there were no monkeys left in the room that had first experienced the cold water spray. Still, none of the new monkeys were allowed to climb up. The other monkeys kept pulling them down. Not one monkey in the room knew why, but none were allowed to get the bananas.

We aren't monkeys, but sometimes we exhibit behaviour that seems rather monkey-like. We don't even remember why; we just know that debt is a part of life and is needed to win in the money game. So we participate in the myths made popular by these companies and banks and financial institutions in particular, and we learn to spout the principles of the myth. As years go by and as we invest more money and time into the myth, we become great disciples and can preach the points of the myth with great fervour. We become such experts on the myth that we can persuade others to join the lie. 'What! You made the full payment yourself and purchased that old model hatchback. You are really old fashioned. You could have taken a bank loan, clubbed it with your money and got yourself that brand new sedan. It looks so good. And that is what everyone who is doing well in their life is driving.'

Luckily, I never joined that lie as I had learnt the lessons about money and personal finance from people like Napoleon Hill and Dr Thomas Stanley early in my career. And working as a banker did help me understand these concepts at the ground level.

Endnotes

1. Stanford Marshmallow Experiment, https://en.wikipedia.org/wiki/Stanford_marshmallow_experiment

Chapter 5

The Real Cost of Borrowing

Now here comes the toughest part. If I have been able to connect with you up to this point, I now stand a chance of losing the connection. Why? It is because I am now going to change you. And when I say this, I really mean to change you for your greater good. And when someone tries to change you without your consent, you will usually retaliate and defend your stance. To avoid this confrontation, I seek your approval to present you something which is not propaganda or bias and marketing gimmick but an important fact which has been kept hidden from the masses so that a particular section of the society benefits from their ignorance.

Your view or belief system, developed over a period of years, learning from your parents, at school, college and the real world outside, comprising banks, credit card companies, jewellers, retailers, real estate developers and so on, is called your paradigm. It is your filter system. If you receive any information in line with your existing belief system then you accept the information. But if you receive information that doesn't match your belief system, you filter it out and usually with it the person who provided you that information. 'He knows nothing and talks trash,' or it may be something like 'I don't believe you. You sound so old-fashioned.'

In the field of psychology, it is also called as *Confirmation Bias*,[1] which simply says that we seek information or interpret data in a way that confirms our pre-existing beliefs or hypothesis. Additionally, we give less weight or even ignore evidence that disagrees with our beliefs.

The scary thing about our paradigm is that it is based on our past and our feelings which many a time are not based on facts. And what if it was wrong? What if our feelings and our past gave us a road map that sent us towards a place that we can't acknowledge, as by doing so we would make a fool of ourselves. So what do we do? We justify our actions. We justify our belief system since we don't want to appear either ignorant or foolish in front of others.

But acting on incorrect information, no matter how deeply held, can be catastrophic. The saying 'what you don't know can't hurt you' is ludicrous. What you don't know can kill you. If you don't know that consuming excessive sugar will make you diabetic and you end up eating too much of it then it doesn't mean you won't get diabetes just because you didn't know it. It doesn't happen that way as ignorance is not always blissful.

In the next few pages, I will be busting certain myths. However, I need to warn you to watch out for your instinct to defend your existing belief system about debts and borrowing. Calm down, relax and go for a ride with me for a few pages. I know that it will be difficult to accept everything at the first go but, having experienced it myself and having lived on the truths and not the myths, I can assure you that once you are able to break the myths, you too will put yourself on the path to progress just as I was able to do so a few years ago. Hence, I suggest that you too put all your biases aside, remove your coloured glasses and read the following pages in a relaxed state with an open mind.

#Myth 1

MYTH	TRUTH
• Debt is a tool and should be used to create prosperity for ourselves.	• Debt is a tool used by the banks, financial institutions to create prosperity for themselves.

How many times per day, on an average, do you receive a call asking if you would like to avail of a personal loan or a credit card? Two to three times per day would be a good guess. And how many times per day do you receive a call asking if you would like to open a PPF account, a Sukanya Samridhi account or whether you would like to know the details about the National Pension System (NPS) or plain term insurance? The answer would be none.

Have you ever wondered why these banks set up such a big team of tele-callers or outsource this operation to some third party just to give you a cold call? It is because banks make money by selling loans to you. These institutions are not worried about your prosperity and hence would never bother to inform you about the benefits of PPF, Sukanya Samridhi, NPS, term insurance, investing in equity and so on. But they are always on their toes and ensure that you take one or the other kind of loan from them because lending money to you ensures a continuous stream of income for them in the form of interest, commissions and fees. As a matter of fact, if you go to any branch of a bank and enquire about PPF, Sukanya Samridhi, term insurance etc, then in most of the cases you will be treated with contempt and be given the last priority as they will be busy selling loans to their other customers.

If you are still not convinced about how debts create prosperity for the lender and worsens the life of the borrower, I would suggest that you watch the Academy award nominated movie *Mother India*. The movie depicts very beautifully how borrowing money leads a family to turmoil they had never expected and how they get trapped into the vicious cycle of debt which results in the loss of the father–son duo. On the other hand, the movie also shows how the lender keeps enjoying his life on the interest income the borrowers bring to him and how he rules over them. The bible proverb, 'The rich rule over the poor, and the borrower is slave to the lender', is not a thing of the past but is also applicable in today's world.

You may say that the movie is five decades old and times have changed. True! Times have changed but the system has not. We still come across news of farmers' suicide. And the primary reason of such suicides is nothing but debt. Seeing their inability to pay back the loans and losing all hope, these hapless farmers commit suicide.

You may also say that farmers commit suicide because they don't have a steady stream of income but 'since you have a steady job' you don't have to worry. Wrong! It is your steady job which encourages the banks to lend you money. They know that the typical salaried middle-class people will not default on their loans and they will do anything, and by 'anything' I really mean anything—work really hard; stay late in office; miss quality time with the family; continue with the job and the boss they don't like; give up their dreams and passion—just to pay back the loan. And that is the reason they like issuing loans to you but not to farmers (as we discussed earlier banks lend loans to farmers mainly because the RBI has told them to do so and the banks need to meet the minimum criteria of 'Priority Sector Lending' if they want to continue their business). The joke that 'if you don't like your job or boss then take a loan' isn't really a joke. It tells a lot but we often ignore its importance thinking that it's just a joke.

While the salaried middle class may not commit suicide like farmers, in reality, they are already dead and have become a machine who wakes up early in the morning and works hard just to pay interest and principal to the lenders and the banks. They have lost their emotions, their desires, their dreams and their passions. And when a person has no emotion, no desire, no dream and no passion, he is as good as dead. I may sound a bit harsh here but the reality is that most of the people don't really live their lives. As someone has rightly said, 'Modern slaves are not in chains but in debts.'

I often tell people that if you want to be like someone, observe them—how they live and what they do. Remember, the best way to change your life is to find people who've already achieved what you want and then emulate their behaviour. If you want to be muscular and physically fit, study physically fit people and their daily routine and habits—what they eat and how much and what kind of exercise they do, etc. Similarly, if you want to be rich, imitate how the rich people deal with money. Simply, do what rich people do and not what the average middle-class people surrounding you tell you to do. The Forbes 400 is a list of the richest 400 people in America as rated by the *Forbes* magazine. And when these richest men were surveyed, 75 per cent of them said the best way to build wealth is to become and stay debt-free. All these people have lived on less than what they earned and spent only when they had cash. They took no credit and never delayed their payments. Remember, when you don't have any payments to be made to banks and credit card companies, then you will have more money to invest and that is how you can become rich.

Henry Ford used to say that debt is a lazy man's method to purchase items and his philosophy was so ingrained in Ford Motor Company that it didn't offer financing (selling cars on credit) until ten years after General Motors did. Now, of course, Ford Motor Credit is one of the most profitable of Ford Motors' operations.

#Myth 2

MYTH	TRUTH
• Debt is a service that banks and financial institutions provide to the people in need.	• Debt is a product sold to people who don't really need it by creating an artificial need for it.

If you go to a shopping mall and browse through various items in an electronic product store and then a salesman comes to you and asks how he can help you, your reply would generally be, 'I am just going through the items and will ask for your assistance in case of need.' Why do we say like that? Because we all know that the store is there for money. They have a product line like TV, laptops, washing machines, mobile sets and refrigerators and if you buy one such product, they make a profit. So we build up sales resistance and say, 'I'm just looking'.

But when we go to a bank, we don't think that they are selling products to us. We feel as if they are providing services to us and we feel indebted to them. The truth is that the banks and other financial institutions don't provide service; rather they sell products and usually services come along with them. And what are those products? Well, they have a long list of such products and it is so long that they can make a catalogue out of them. And the product line includes savings account, current account, fixed deposit, credit card, debit card, home loan, car loan, personal loan, gold loan, loan against property, commercial loan, education loan and all these products once sold to a customer like you and me bring profit to the bank.

And that is why almost all the employees of the bank are trained to sell the products. Just try to visit any bank with a request to open a simple fixed deposit or a savings account and while your request will be honoured, you will be bombarded with information on various banking products such as insurance, loans, unit linked insurance plans (ULIPs) etc. and how the bank is committed to increase the wealth for its customer and how they care for their customers' prosperity. Cross-selling is what this is called in the banking community. And what does this cross-selling mean? It simply means that if a customer asks for one product, sell them five instead.

The reality is that these bank officers have a target to meet so that the bank's profit increases and they are just doing their duty. They have a target for cross-selling as well. And when you take financial advice from a bank officer, a stock broker or a wealth manager, remember that they are taught and trained more in selling the bank's products—products which will increase the bank's profit and not yours—and less on choosing the right investment tools for you.

Having been part of the banking system for nearly six years, I have witnessed how things work and how they don't. Also, there is a joke that the bankers share. It says that a bank is a place where you could borrow money if you could prove you don't need it. And that is what is happening. It is actually lending money to people like you and me—the typical salaried middle-class people who don't really need the loans except for a few cases such as a home loan.

And when the bank feels that you need a loan, it won't give it to you easily until and unless it assures itself that its loan will get repaid. For example, it won't lend to farmers and small traders and businessman so easily. And it won't lend to people who need money urgently if they don't have a steady stream of income. I am not saying that banks are evil and they don't lend to people in need and you should stay away from them. In fact, it is their duty to see the credit worthiness of its borrowers because it is the public money which they are lending and they need to ensure that the money they lend comes back to them with added interest. If any loan goes bad, the bank's capital is lost and with it the people who had deposited their money with the bank suffer. And if a bank really loses a big chunk of money then it is the tax payers' money—our money—which the government uses to revitalise the bank.[2] This is the reason the RBI has prescribed rules under which a bank can give loans to people.

However, the notion that a bank does some kind of noble service is wrong. It operates with the sole purpose of making money by selling debt products to people.

What happens with the selling of such debt products? We end up buying many of them; in other words, we borrow money. We borrow money not just because it is made easy for us, but because we are sold on the convenience, perceived prosperity and fun that all that material stuff and associated debt are supposed to bring for us.

#Myth 3

MYTH	TRUTH
• If no one used debt, our economy would collapse.	• Rather, it would prosper.

Whenever I have told my fellow bankers that people should avoid availing of loans, they have protested saying that if that happens then our economy would collapse. The money-multiplier effect would come down; there would be less churning of money and businesses will stagnate. While all these factors may seem slightly technical to some of you, there is nothing to worry about. What my friends and people who have undergone a university level course in finance and economics suspect is purely theoretical and doesn't work in the real world.

However, let's pretend for some time that my book reaches the hands of earning Indians and wisdom prevails over them and they stop taking loans over the next ten years. Will the economy collapse? No. It would prosper, although banks and other lenders would have to find other avenues to make more profit.

Just imagine what people would do if they didn't have any payments to make. They would save and they would spend. They would not support banks and make their shareholders rich. The amount saved by the people when invested would be routed to the economy only in the form of purchase of company shares or in the form of government/municipal/corporate bonds. This would help the company (whose shares were purchased) prosper and help the government authority to build better infrastructure. And what happens when the companies of our economy prosper and there is better infrastructure? The economy prospers and its citizens get a better and healthier lifestyle.

Secondly, spending by debt-free people would further support and make the economy prosper. As the noted author Dave Ramsey says, 'When people start spending without availing of debt, the economy would be much more stable without the tidal waves caused by "consumer confidence" or the lack thereof.' If the consumers were out of debt and living within their means, the confidence the economy would have in them would be much more and the companies would continue manufacturing products. You should understand that with no debt, spending doesn't stop. Spending will continue; though people will defer their purchases till they have accumulated enough cash for it. And once people have accumulated wealth through their savings and investments, the spending will also increase and the economy will prosper further.

Additionally, since people would be debt-free and living within their means, they will have surplus which they may use towards charity after investing a part of it. The invested money will go to the companies to improve and increase their operations and profit and to the government which will use the money to build better infrastructure. People will then have hospitals and schools funded by their own money and dependency on government funds will come down. This will help the government come out of the welfare business, reduce various kinds of subsidies and it will focus more on governance. Subsequently, taxes will come down and we will have even more wealth at our disposal.

You may think that I am throwing up a very rosy picture and such a utopian society is not possible. Well, I am not sure whether such a society is possible in the near future, but I am sure that with no debt,[3] the economy will not collapse, but rather it would prosper. And I am also sure that when you stop availing of a loan of any kind, you too will prosper.

#Myth 4

MYTH	TRUTH
• We should take advantage of leverage by availing of a loan.	• Leverage brings considerable risk and reduces all its advantages.

Once I was talking to some of my friends on the disadvantages of debt. So one of my friends, with an MBA said to me, 'Abhishek, you are a finance major and working as a corporate banker. How come you are missing the leverage part? Wouldn't it be beneficial to take a loan as it allows us to do and achieve things which we would not be able to do and gain without it?' My answer to such questions which I often encounter is strictly a 'no'.

For all the non-finance background people, let me give you a small introduction to what exactly leverage is. Suppose a company is formed with a capital of ₹100 from its promoters and investors.

The company has an equity of ₹100 and this is the money it will use to run its operations. Assume the company's operation has a return on capital (ROC) of 15 per cent. The total value of the company is ₹115 at the end of the first year.

Now let us assume that the company uses debt and avails bank loan of ₹200 at the interest rate of 10 per cent. The company will now have a total capital of ₹300 to invest in its business. And at the end of the year it would have made ₹345—remember the ROC is 15 per cent. After paying back the loan of ₹200 and the interest cost of ₹20, the company will have total remaining amount of ₹125. Hence the company's value in this case is more than what it would have been when it hadn't availed of any bank loan. And this is what people call 'leverage'.

However, leverage comes with greater risk. If an investor uses leverage to make an investment and the investment moves against the investor, say, instead of an ROC of 15 per cent, the actual ROC was 8 per cent, his or her loss would be much greater than it would've been if the investment had not been leveraged. Hence, always remember that leverage magnifies both gains and losses and the belief that leverage is always beneficial is wrong.

Now let's get back to our original discussion. Whenever people talk about the advantage of leverage, seldom is the risk factor bought into the formula. And, what is the risk with leverage for an individual? It is the same as it is for a corporate, that is, when the assumed ROC from the investments that you made on the borrowed money is less than the borrowing cost, you make a loss. Also while the borrowing cost is fixed, that is, the interest that you have to pay to the bank is fixed, the return that you would get from your investments—stocks, mutual funds, real estate, gold etc.—is variable. So there is a very high probability, almost 50 per cent, that your ROC will be less than your borrowing cost. And this is the risk you take when you try to take advantage of leverage.

In the investment world and the academia, there is a statistical measure of risk called 'Beta' which measures the volatility of the investment tool. A big beta means a big risk. So when you are trying to take advantage of leverage, understand that you carry a 'high beta' with you and hence a risk that you may not be able to earn the return which is in excess of the interest that you need to return to the bank from which you have taken a loan.

Additionally, people rarely bring taxation into the picture when they talk about the leverage. Assume you borrowed ₹1 lakh at 10 per cent, you would pay ₹10,000 to the bank in the form of interest per annum. Assume, you invested this ₹1 lakh and made a return of say 14 per cent. You would make a net income of ₹4000 (net interest paid to the bank). However, there is a tax element that is yet to be added on the net earnings. If you are in the 30 per cent tax bracket, you will pay ₹2800 in taxes (20 per cent capital gain tax on ₹14000 of interest income) if you had invested at capital gain rates. You will therefore not net ₹4000 but only ₹1200. Do you still think it is worth taking the risk?

And if you take into account the risk factor and taxes together, the perceived yield of the leverage will come down drastically. All the finance graduates and bankers, people with vested interests, want to cross swords on this issue but I think they will find that a reasonable risk factor reduces the advantage of leverage to zero if viewed closely and minutely.

I will give you an example of how banks use the concept of risk in their lending business. Usually before lending to a corporate, the bank will assess the perceived ROC from its lending. Lending by the bank is nothing but an investment from the bank's perspective as it brings in more money to it in the form of interest paid by the borrowing entity. However, not all corporates are equally creditworthy, that is, a company with a huge cash surplus and a sound and robust business model is more likely to pay back the loan than a company which doesn't have cash and is running entirely on debt. So lending to a cash-rich company is less risky than lending to a company which doesn't have much capital of its own. And to incorporate this risk, banks don't use ROC; rather they use Risk-Adjusted-Return on Capital, called RAROC by adding additional factors. It is ironical that while a bank uses the risk factor internally in its investments, seldom does it teach the risk associated with the leverage and borrowing to its individual customers.

Another misconception that is popular among the masses is that they think 'leverage' is equivalent to 'availing of loan'. Leverage is not only taking a loan; rather it is taking a loan and putting it to some use such as investments or business, where you expect to get more return than the borrowing cost. And if you are taking a loan say for purchase of a car or for your foreign vacation, then you are not using 'leverage' but simply taking a loan and consuming that borrowed money.

Also, it is very difficult for a common man to take advantage of leverage. Yes, there are seasoned investors and people whose primary profession is advisory and investments and who may be able to reap benefits from the leverage, but my advice for the common folk would be not to get swayed away by the perceived advantage of leverage.

#Myth 5

MYTH	TRUTH
• We should take a loan as it provides a tax benefit to us.	• It is equivalent to saying we should fall sick so that our sick leave doesn't go waste.

It is one of the biggest selling points used by the banks and financial institutions to sell their debt products to us. And in most of the cases we buy their idea and ultimately their product. First of all, we should understand that not all loans provide tax advantage to us. Yes, home loan and education loan do provide a tax relief to us but other loans like auto loans, personal loans,[4] credit card etc. do not provide any kind of tax relief.

Now you may think why there is a difference in tax benefit among loans. It is because the government considers home and education as necessities and hence provides some kind of tax benefit while other loans such as auto loan, personal loan and credit card are considered as purchase of luxury items and hence no tax benefit is provided.

Let us understand what benefit home and education loans really provide. First of all, for education loan, only the interest paid is tax deductible and there is no exemption for the principal part. So you get tax benefit only on the interest paid during the year for your education loan.

Coming to home loan, if you want to avail of the tax benefits from it, then you need to satisfy various conditions before you actually get any benefit. I will put down some of the relevant conditions to highlight how much tax benefit an average buyer gets from a home loan.

- The property should be self-occupied. Hence if you have purchased an under-construction property by availing of a home loan then until your home is completed (and your builder has handed over the completion certificate to you), you cannot claim any tax benefit. Also while the interest paid during the construction period is tax deductible in retrospective, there is no deduction available for the principal amount paid during the construction period.
- The interest paid on the self-occupied property is tax deductible under Sec 24 for a maximum amount of ₹2 lakh. The principal amount paid is tax deductible under Sec 80C. And since in most of the cases, people

already fill the bucket of Sec 80C with PPF, EPF, NSC, Tax Saving FD, ELSS etc., they are unable to take any benefit for the principal amount paid for the home loan. Hence, in almost all the cases, you will get benefit only for the interest paid, just like in education loan.

- Since in most the cases, people avail of a home loan in excess of ₹50 lakh (that is the present situation in most of the Tier-I and Tier-II cities) and since the home loan interest rate is around 9 to 10 per cent, so out of total interest paid of ₹5 lakh, you get benefit for the interest amount paid to the extent of ₹2 lakh only. For the balance and the major part of interest, you do not get any tax benefit.

So getting the tax benefit for home loan is not so easy and straightforward as it is perceived by the general masses. However, no bank/FI will tell you about these conditions when they are selling debt products (loans) to you. They will tell that you will get tax benefit, so you buy their idea and ultimately their product, (debt product) and end up paying more than what you had earlier calculated. You feel cheated if you are tracking and managing your EMI payments diligently. But again you can't do much as you have already made the purchase and can't reverse it so easily.

- Also while you are able to get tax benefit on the interest paid on the home loan, you should understand that the real benefit is not really worth going in for loans. If you are not convinced then let's do some maths. Assume a typical salaried middle-class person has taken a home loan of ₹50 lakh—a very conservative amount in the present—and is paying a yearly interest of ₹5 lakh (the interest amount will come down with the payment of the principal but will not differ much in the initial part of the loan repayment until and unless the person is prepaying the loan in bulk).

Assuming this person to be under the 30 per cent bracket (if he is under 20 per cent bracket the benefit will be much less), he gets tax deduction of ₹60,000 (30 per cent of ₹2 lakh) by paying an interest of ₹5 lakh. All and all, his net pay out is ₹4.40 lakh.

- So how on earth does availing of loan become beneficial for a person? We are paying ₹4.40 lakh per annum simply as interest payment to the bank and we think that we are doing a wise thing by availing of the loan. Wrong! Your interest payment is nothing but an expense for you and income for the bank. If anything is going out of your pocket, it is making you poorer by that amount. Telling us that we should avail of a home loan since it provides tax relief is akin to saying it is better to consume 4.4 ml of poison than to take 5 ml of poison as it will not affect our health that much. Poison, whether it is 4.4 ml or 5 ml, is going to harm you and if you continue consuming it, then it will kill you. In a slightly moderate tone, it is akin to saying that I should fall sick as it will help me avail of the sick leave being provided by my organisation.

I am not saying you shouldn't take an education loan or a home loan at all. What I am saying is that availing of any loan just because it gives you peanuts for tax benefit is a wrong idea. However, the banks have been able to sell this idea and that is why people love to take loans and banks are more than happy to give them.

#Myth 6

MYTH	TRUTH
• Taking a longer tenure loan is beneficial as the EMI feels easy on my pocket.	• A longer tenure loan depletes you of your savings and brings considerable income to the bank.

Once I was reading an article which went something like this, 'Good news for home loan borrowers as banks are increasing the loan tenure by ten more years thereby easing the EMI payments the homebuyers would make.' I wondered whether it was really good news for the customers or for the banks. I did some calculation and found out the truth and realised that the actual headline of the article should have been: 'Good news for banks and lending institutes as they are increasing the loan tenure by ten more years thereby making more money for themselves for every loan they extend.'

Seeing that retail customers are already tying up their monthly income with EMIs of cars, home appliances and furniture, banks thought it would be difficult for them to sell their biggest asset, their best product, home loan, to them if they didn't increase the tenure of the home loans. So they have started selling their home loan with the tag line—pay your home loan with easy EMIs by availing of our thirty years tenure loan. And what did the people do? They fell into the trap without realising how much more they would actually pay by going for a longer tenure loan.

So here is the math for you. When you take a loan of ₹50 lakh at an interest rate of 9 per cent, then with a fifteen-year tenure of loan, your EMI comes to ₹50,713. However, when the tenure is increased to thirty years, the EMI gets reduced to ₹40,231 and we feel happy about it thinking that we can easily afford to take that loan (and with it the home) as the EMI fits our pocket. Most people usually miss the point that with the longer tenure, they keep on paying the bank for a longer period and when the loan is closed they actually end up paying much more than what they would have paid, had they gone for a shorter term loan. So, in this case for a loan of ₹50 lakh, they would have paid a total of

₹91 lakh had they gone for a fifteen-year loan. However, with a thirty-year loan, they end up paying an amount of ₹1.45 crore. Imagine, paying a total of ₹1.45 crore for a loan of ₹50 lakh. Where did this nearly ₹1 crore go? It went to the bank as interest income. And who paid it? You, of course.

Loan Availed: ₹50 Lakh; **Interest Rate:** 9% p.a.			
Tenor	**EMI Per Month**	**No of Payments**	**Total Payment**
30 Years	40,231	360	1,44,83,160
15 Years	50,713	180	91,28,340
Difference	**10,482**		**53,54,820**

So, just by showing you a reduced EMI—difference being as low as ₹10,000—the banks end up earning ₹53 lakh more per customer. And what if there are lakhs and crores of such customers? Well, you can do the math now and understand how much money banks make by simply extending the tenure of the loans for their customers.

Be careful of the bank or the real estate broker who urges you to go for a thirty-year loan. In my opinion, thirty-year home loans are for people who enjoy slavery so much that they want to extend their loans for fifteen more years and pay lakhs and crores of rupees more for the privilege.

I am not saying you shouldn't take a home loan at all. What I am trying to drive home is the point that taking a longer tenure loan is simply stupidity and thinking that the reduced EMI will fit into your income makes you go for something which you shouldn't have gone for. Never, I repeat, never go for more than a fifteen-year home loan. If the EMI doesn't fit your income then instead of increasing the tenure of the loan, reduce the amount of loan that you would take. But never go for a longer tenure loan.

#Myth 7

MYTH	TRUTH
• The interest rate as quoted by my bank is what I am paying.	• You don't pay the quoted interest rate but a rate which is more than what the banks quote.

Having studied finance for MBA at IIM Kozhikode and during my Master's of Financial Engineering at University of California, Los Angeles (UCLA) helped me understand certain simple things which are mostly ignored by the masses, in addition to making me ready for a career in the field of finance. One such thing that I studied during my Investment class was the concept of Annual Percentage Rate (APR) and Effective Annual Rate (EAR).

Let us understand what these are and how they impact you. When banks say that they are offering you a home loan at 12 per cent p.a. (I know home loan rate is around 9 per cent p.a. but I am assuming it at 12 per cent to simplify the calculation), what they are quoting is the APR. As you are paying interest every month on your home loan, the banks divide this APR by 12 (number of months in a year) to arrive at the monthly interest rate which in this case comes to 1 per cent. Now since your home loan is compounded monthly, the real interest rate also known as EAR that you pay is 1 per cent compounded over the period of twelve months which comes to 12.70 per cent.

So while you thought that you took the loan at the rate of 12 per cent p.a, the real rate actually was 12.70 per cent. You may think what harm could this small amount of 0.7 per cent really do? Well when it comes to home loan, where the loan amount is high and the maturity period is long, even a small amount of 0.7 per cent can cause a big difference. Not convinced? Let's do the math.

Loan Availed: ₹50 Lakh; **Tenor:** 20 years				
Interest Rate	**EMI Per Month**	**Principal Payment**	**Interest Payment**	**Total Payment**
12.00%	55,054	50,00,000	82,13,034	1,32,13,034
12.70%	57,513	50,00,000	88,03,239	1,38,03,239
Difference	**2,459**	0	**5,90,205**	**5,90,205**

So, in this case a small difference of 0.7 per cent in the interest rate is causing you to pay nearly ₹6 lakh more to the bank. And when you compare this amount of ₹6 lakh to the original amount of ₹50 lakh that you had initially taken, you will realise the impact the small interest rate differences can cause.

So, next time you go to the bank to avail of a home loan, ask them for the EAR that you would be actually paying and don't simply buy this loan at what the bank is offering you to sell.

If Loan is Such a Bad Product Then Why is It Being Sold?

Let me tell you something very clearly here. Banks are not bad and neither are the debt products. Banks are often called the backbone of any economy and they play a major role in the growth and development of the economy and the society at large. They have a much wider role than simply accepting deposits and lending money to people. But since here we are discussing personal finance, we have restricted ourselves to deposits and lending because that is how most of us interact with the banks and it is these two transactions which affect our pockets directly.

Now coming to the point that if debt is such a bad product then why is it being sold? Rather, why it is being allowed to be sold. Well, debt is not a bad product in the first place. It was created so that people or a business entity in genuine need of capital could borrow money from a standard platform and pay it back once they had been able to fulfil their need. It is the loan which lets a company generate much more profit than what they could do if they didn't have access to it. Similarly, it is the loan which lets students pursue their dream of higher education and it is the loan which helps most of the people buy a home.

It is not the use of loan that is affecting us; rather it is its abuse which is impacting normal people like you and me. With the growth of the economy and rise in disposable income among the masses, banks and financial institutions saw an opportunity to make money by lending it to people. And as the greed increased in these institutions, they started marketing their loan products in such a way so as to lure more and more gullible people to avail of them.

Not to sound like a broken record, but banks and debt as such are not bad at all. They help people who are in need of money and provide a platform to people to earn interest on their surplus. The only problem with debt products is the way they have been marketed and sold among the people. Instead of using them as the last resort, people have started using them as the first opportunity and in most of the cases they are using them even when they don't have to resort to them at all.

Make the Bank Your Growth Partner

Instead of allowing your banks to rob you of your money, you should learn to make them your growth partner. The idea with which the banking system was set up was to help the people and economy prosper. But when greed creeps into the banks, then they use their greed to inflate the greed of the people and start making money. However, when this greed of the banks crosses a threshold, the entire economy suffers and both banks as well as the people lose their money and sleep.

We all know how the sub-prime crisis had hit the entire world and not only people of the developed economy suffered but many people from the developing world like India lost their jobs just because some greedy bankers decided to lend money to people who were equally greedy and not in a position to repay the loans. The loans were not prime (good) loans, so the bankers themselves classified them to be sub-prime loans, hoping some miracle would happen so that all these greedy people returned them on time. But that didn't happen. Broke and greedy people didn't repay the loans and the banks themselves had to pay the price which resulted in some of the biggest banks, which had survived over a century, to close their operations.

You should understand that just like debts, banks are not bad. They are here to help you. They have some of the 'less marketed' wonderful products and provide avenues through which you can invest your money which can make it appreciate and grow. The only thing is that with the present competition among the banks and to make their stock prices soar, they are in a mindless race to increase their asset size and that is the reason they are catching every Tom, Dick and Harry to lend money to. Do not let yourself become their next Tom, Dick or Harry.

Remember, your largest wealth-building asset is your income. When you tie up your future income (for repayment of loans), you lose. When you invest your income, you win and become wealthy and can do anything you want. You should understand that debt doesn't give you freedom, rather it enslaves you. To have savings, a surplus in your bank account is freedom. Savings means freedom from debt. Money in the bank account means the freedom to leave your job if the boss is intolerable or the benefits and/or the growth path have been curtailed. And if you lose your job, having savings is the freedom to keep your house and car because you can cover your payments, if you have any to make in the first place. Having savings means you can start a business of your own or buy land. And having savings will enable you to turn your hobby into your profession. And when do you have savings and surplus? It is when you start saying no to loans. A wise man once told me, 'You become rich not when you are able to afford big loans. You become rich when you are able to say no to loans.'

Endnotes

1. What is Confirmation Bias?, https://www.psychologytoday.com/us/blog/science-choice/201504/what-is-confirmation-bias
2. Whenever you hear the news that the government is putting in some XYZ crore of rupees in a bank, then understand that the recipient bank has lost money by lending money to wrong people and corporates and it is the normal taxpayers' money which is being used to bring back the bank to its normal operation.
3. The reference here is to personal debt and not corporate debt. Corporates are able to tap into better investment opportunities with debt and they save money on tax as all the loans they avail of are tax deductible. However, not all personal loans are tax deductible, for example personal loans, auto loans and credit card loans are not tax deductible.
4. Personal loan, if availed of for business purpose, is tax deductible. For any other purpose there is no tax benefit.

Chapter 6

The Mouse Trap

After making profits for the bank and themselves by selling loans to people of the town and closing the books for the previous financial year, Thakur and Mohan were having a discussion one afternoon after their lunch. While Mohan was feeling elated to have made substantial wealth in a very short period of time, Thakur was grim and thoughtful during the conversation.

Thakur: So Mohan, how does it feel?

Mohan: Feels great Sir! We have made much more profit than what we had envisaged.

Thakur: That's correct. But I see one problem in the way we are lending our money.

Mohan: And what is that?

Thakur: Presently, we are lending money to people for the purchase of cattle, cart and materials. We are also lending to people for the construction of their homes. However, all this is one-time lending.

Mohan: What does one-time lending mean?

Thakur: This type of lending happens only once. Say a person takes a loan from us for the construction of his house. Once his house his completed and he pays back our loan, then the income stream which we were earning from this loan, stops. Similarly, if someone takes a loan from us for the purchase of a bullock cart then once he pays back the loan, we stop earning from that particular loan.

Mohan: True. Most of these are one-time expenses by the people. But how can we force somebody to construct another house or purchase another bullock cart? If we need to earn more, we need to lend more.

Thakur: That we will be doing. I was thinking that if we could make people borrow money for their day-to-day items like vegetables, groceries, clothes, shoes etc., then we would not have to worry about the closure of the loan. People would be purchasing these things on a continuous basis, and if they get into the habit of buying these things on loan, then all we would have to do is to sit, relax and enjoy the interest they would bring to us throughout their life.

Mohan: But how is that possible? Usually these items are priced low and hence the interest will be very little.

Thakur: Well, it is very much possible. You must have observed that the shopkeepers who sell these day-to-day items first insist on coins and if the customer doesn't have coins then they sell the goods on credit. It is equivalent to shopkeepers giving loan to the customer who uses that borrowed money to purchase the items. So, the notion that people don't purchase these day-to-day trivial items on borrowed money is false. They do it on a regular basis. The only thing is that these loans are extended by shopkeepers and not by banks.

Mohan: It makes sense. I never thought of it in that way.

Thakur: Well, shopkeepers do that for a particular purpose. They know that when they sell their goods on credit, people usually buy more than what they would if they had to pay with coins. They know that every individual has limited means but unlimited desires. And when they provide credit, they entice the customers to fulfil some of their desires by giving an illusion of enhanced means. And in this way, their sales increase and they make more profit as people end up buying more goods from them.

Mohan: Correct. But how do we come into the picture?

Thakur: Well, we can do one thing. We will tell these shopkeepers to forward us the bills and we will reimburse them. In that way all these merchants and shopkeepers will get their money immediately. We will become the lender and the customer will pay us the money and we will be making money by earning interest.

Mohan: Do you think this system will work?

Thakur: I am more than convinced that it will work. First, the shopkeepers will get their money immediately and they will not have to follow up with their customers to collect their dues. And since they will be able to sell more goods on credit, we could demand a part of the income from them as commission. We will be making money in two ways: One, as the commission sold on all goods on credit. Second, we will be charging interest to the customers as they will be borrowing money from us.

Mohan: Brilliant. It's a win-win situation for us and the shopkeepers. We will be able to make profit from commission as well as interest. And the shopkeepers would be able to sell more goods and receive their money promptly. The customers will be the only losers since they are being enticed to purchase goods which they cannot afford and their future income will get tied up to pay us the money.

Thakur: Yes. But we do not need to worry about the well-being of customers. We only need to think about ourselves. We can project this in such a way that people purchasing goods on credit would consider themselves as smart and intelligent and people using coins will think that they are old-fashioned.

Mohan: And the best part is that these are not one-time loans. These loans will never be paid off completely as people will get habituated to using credit. And we will have a lifetime of continuous income in the form of commission and interest.

Thakur: You are getting smarter. So let's go and talk to all the shopkeepers in town. We shouldn't waste any time.

Welcome to the World of Credit Card

Probably you would have guessed by now what I am coming to. Yes, I want you to say no to any credit card so as to live a debt-free, peaceful and fruitful life. And it is the easiest thing to start your journey on a financially blissful life or wait, which is probably the hardest thing to do.

Many experts have written multiple articles on the evils of the credit card (there are equal number of articles written by a group of people with vested interests on how a credit card allows you to use others' money, at zero interest cost too). People who speak from the consumers' point of view—and not from the bank's (financial institution) say that credit cards are one of the most horrible financial tools. The convenience of the plastic makes you buy stuff which you would never buy otherwise. The advertisements show that you will have a better social status, glamour and fun by using their gold, titanium and platinum cards. Well, if your self-esteem is drawn from the 'metal' of the plastic in your hand, then you really need to reconsider your priorities in life.

Credit cards were designed initially as a loyalty card in the form of Diners Card and Travel Card and were issued by departmental stores, restaurants and travel companies. Later banks and other financial institutions saw an opportunity to make money and started issuing credit cards which could be used anywhere and everywhere. And then the propaganda started—how the credit card gives you social status, the freedom to purchase anything and how they would help you to improve your lifestyle. Steadily and slowly, people started falling for these gimmicks and they bought the ideas sold by the banks and ultimately bought the debt products and credit cards from them. Well, it is not only you and me but the entire generation of the present who have been sold—sold on making banks and credit card companies rich.

Once I was speaking to my friend who used to carry four to five credit cards and told him how the credit card was ruining our financial lives and overall life in general. He replied that it was not ruining his life, rather it had made it better. The credit card gave him reward points, air miles, cashback on every purchase which he didn't get with the use of cash and a debit card. He also said that the credit card allowed him to use other people's money at zero interest cost and in this way he was able to save money.

Additionally, since my friend is also a corporate banker, he is aware of the high interest cost of nearly 35–40 per cent on a credit card (many people are not aware of such a high interest cost) which a user has to pay if he is not able to make the payment on time. When I asked him, 'What if your expenses increase on the continuous usage of your credit card and you are not able to make the payment on time? Will you not have to pay high interest to the bank?' He replied, 'I am disciplined when it comes to the usage of the credit card and I control my expenses. Also, I always make my payment on time so there is no question of interest payment to the bank.' Apparently, my friend was sold big time on the idea of borrowing money by using a credit card.

The so-called theoretical merits of the credit card, as shared by everyone, is what credit card companies and banks want you to believe and that is how they have been able to bring almost the entire working population to use their products. If all people believed that by using other people's money at zero cost, they are able to save money and since this notion is being shared by everyone—I emphasise that not many people on this planet would say that they are not disciplined and they are paying huge interest cost by delaying their payments—shouldn't all the banks and credit card companies be making losses as they are lending money at zero cost? Well, the reality is that these companies are not making losses; rather they are making huge profits and those profits are nothing but the commission and interest they are earning. And who is paying the commission and interest? We are!

Additionally, credit card companies (including banks issuing credit cards) make money from other sources as well. I have listed the main sources of the earning of credit card companies and banks issuing credit cards so that you know how your money is being used to make these companies rich.

- Fees (annual fees, late fees, over-the-limit fees, cash-advance fees). Usually the fees are low and in some cases nil in the first year but increase substantially from the second year onwards. Since credit card companies need to bring you into their net, they offer fantastic discounts initially and once you get habituated to using the card they start charging you in the form of various fees. In addition to the above fees, they levy dormancy charges in case you stop using the credit card for a while. So it is a win-win game for them. You use my credit card, I earn money. You don't use my credit card, I earn money. In either case, I win and you lose.
- Interest on revolving debt we carry with them. Whenever we make the minimum payment and not the full amount,

we start paying interest at the rate of 35–40 per cent p.a. (which is very high considering the average interest rate on almost all loans range from 10–15 per cent) on the outstanding amount to the banks and credit card companies. And this interest is not calculated from your payment date. Rather it is calculated from the date of your initial purchase. So the credit card companies trick you by saying that you can pay the minimum amount and continue using the card; in that way they make lots of money in the form of the huge interest rate.

- A cut of the purchase price from the merchants we make our purchases from. Remember the merchants and credit card companies have a tie-up. So whenever you purchase items using your credit card, a part of your money also goes to the credit card companies.
- Commission from selling cardholders' names to others so more people can hawk their cards and wares at us.

Time to Bust Myths

All the theoretical merits of the usage of credit cards have been marketed and propagated by the banks and credit card companies in such a way that they have somewhat become urban legends. They are being accepted by almost everyone as the 'universal and eternal truth'. But, it is time to dispel these myths and I want you to read the following pages with an open mind. Put all your biases and prejudices aside and read with an open heart.

#Myth 8

MYTH	TRUTH
• I earn brownie points such as cashback, air miles, and reward points on the use of credit card.	• You can't earn money by spending money.

If you have gone fishing or have observed someone fishing, then you would know that to catch fish, you need to entice them with a bait without which you won't be able to catch them. Banks and credit card companies know this fact very well and that is why they have been able to lure everyone to use their card by offering baits in the form of cashback, air miles and reward points. They know that if they want to earn ₹100 from someone, they need to offer ₹1 as freebies to them. After all, who doesn't like freebies? And if it is the typical salaried middle-class people then these companies can sell them a product of ₹1 lakh by offering a freebie of ₹500. And the best part is that they have been very successful in this strategy.

Well, the fact is that you can't earn money by spending money. You get all these freebies only when you have spent a considerable amount of money using the credit card and that is what they want you to do. If I am able to get a cashback of ₹500 by spending ₹20,000 then I didn't save or earn ₹500; rather I have spent ₹19,500.

You may now question that since I have some fixed expense every month (such as groceries, fuel etc.), why can't I make those payments using the credit card and earn points. To this I would simply say that I have never seen anybody become rich by earning reward points and cashback but I have witnessed many who have fallen into the debt-trap on continuous use of credit card. The millionaires don't get rich with free hats, brownie points and air miles. So what do they do? They use cash or debit card. And what do middle-class people do? They use credit cards.

There are a set of people who like freebies so much that they can spend money using the credit card just to earn reward points. And in case a person is in dilemma whether to spend money or not, these freebies will act as an enticer and the person will end up spending his hard-earned money and will justify his act by saying, 'See, I have earned so many reward points.' To these people, I would just like to show the real picture.

- *Free deals on cards*: A premium card (which comes at a very high cost—in the sense that you really need to spend a lot of money to get those cards) may provide various offers from free flights to dining discounts to access to airport lounges. However, most of these come with conditions, usually a minimum amount that you need to spend. Further, in case of free flight tickets, only the base fare is waived; the taxes and surcharge remain intact. And since taxes and surcharge constitute a major part of your flight ticket, you may not actually be saving a lot as you are made to believe.
- *Reward point redemption*: Banks charge for redeeming your hard-earned points (since you had to work really hard to earn money and then to spend it to earn those points) too. Hence, converting these points into gifts or vouchers comes with an added price. Second, you can't keep hoarding them endlessly since most points are valid for one to three years. Also, studies have shown that most of the people don't redeem these points as they are busy spending money to collect more points. Makes sense for the credit card companies to offer baits which they don't actually have to pay. I too, when I was using a credit card, had missed enchasing reward points. But not any more as I don't have any to redeem.

Remember, it's all about habit. Just like smoking starts with one or two cigarettes per day and you think you can control it but later realise that you are smoking ten to twelve cigarettes every day and can't say no to it. Similarly it is with the credit card. The banks and credit card companies want you to start using their card by offering baits and they know that once the customer gets habituated to its usage, they will be unable to say no and it would become a part of his life.

#Myth 9

MYTH	TRUTH
• If you pay off your credit card every month, you get the free use of someone else's money at zero interest cost.	• Even if you pay off your credit cards every month; you end up spending more money.

This is the biggest justification (or excuse) given by people when questioned as to why they use a credit card. Everybody, and I really mean everybody, says that they pay off their credit card dues every month on time. In this way, they don't need to pay any interest and hence they are able to use someone else's money at zero cost. I really wonder if everyone says so then how come all these banks and credit card companies make money and why they spend millions on the promotion and advertisement of their products. They aren't here for some community service or are running some public-welfare scheme. They are here for making profit and they are doing so right under your nose giving you a false impression that it is you, the customer, who benefits from the use of their products.

Even if you do pay your credit card bills on time, the fact is that you buy more when using plastic. Studies have shown that a typical grocery purchase almost doubles when the shopper uses plastic.[1] You see no cash pass from your hand, and so you register very little emotional realisation that you've spent money. Many people tell me that they can control their expenses when using a credit card. Therapists specialising in addictions tell us that the first level of treatment always involves denial, which they consider to be a strong indicator that there is an addiction problem.

Now let us assume that you really buy what you need using your credit card and there is no extra purchase. Let us see how much you are really able to save per month by using other people's money. Usually a person in urban and metro centres carries a monthly average debt of ₹10,000 on his credit card. So by using someone else's money at zero interest cost, this person is able to earn the interest earned on the saving account (if he would have paid using cash or debit card, money from his saving account would have been spent). Since the saving account offers an average of 5 per cent p.a. this person is able to save ₹500 (5 per cent of ₹10,000) per year by using the credit card. And if we calculate the saving per month then it comes to the saving of ₹42 per month. Do you still think that by using someone else's money, you are making money? If so, then think again.

#Myth 10

MYTH	TRUTH
• You need a credit card to do online transactions.	• A debit card will do all that.

Whenever I ask people to make cash payment for their monthly expenses, they ask: What about the online transactions? What about the movie tickets, travel tickets or purchasing certain items on the e-com portals? Won't they need a credit card to do all these transactions?

To this, my reply has always been, 'Your debit card will do the same thing for you.' With debit cards your account gets automatically debited and you feel a pain (though slightly lesser when compared to the pain that you register while passing the cash) seeing your account balance coming down. This forces you to be disciplined in your spending habit as you will know that you have only a particular amount of money in your account to last you for the month.

Remember, while debit cards won't earn you reward points or air miles, it will also never put you in a debt trap.

#Myth 11

MYTH	TRUTH
• I can purchase big-ticket items such as LED TVs, sofas etc. using credit card and convert it into an EMI. This way I can save myself from applying for a loan and paying interest.	• Your credit card is already a loan and by converting your payments into an EMI, you pay very high interest cost.

I have seen people purchasing big-ticket consumer goods or furniture using their credit card and then later converting the credit card bill into an EMI spread over say six months or twelve months. Why do people convert a credit card bill into an EMI? It is simply because they are unable to pay the entire bill on time and they are on the verge of default. A bad and embarrassing situation and a sign that the person is losing control of his financial life.

And why do banks provide such a facility? It is because they know that since the person is on the verge of default, it is better to provide him an option to repay the amount over a period of time than to let him default. While defaulting on the credit card bill will bring down the CIBIL score drastically and make it difficult for the person to avail any kind of loan in the future; the credit card companies and banks are not worried about that. They are worried of getting their money back and by providing the EMI option, they are able to get their money back over a period of time.

Let us understand why it is a bad idea to convert the credit card bill into an EMI. First of all, when you convert the bill into EMI, an interest is charged over the outstanding amount. While this interest rate (20-24 per cent) is lower than the usual credit card interest rate (35-40 per cent), it is still very high as compared to the normal interest rate prevailing in the market. Second, you need to pay a processing fees (hidden fees which are not so obviously told to the consumers but are printed in very small fonts somewhere in the long list of 'Terms and Conditions') when you convert your bill into an EMI. And to top it up, you need to pay tax on the processing fees. So even in cases where there is no interest charged on converting the bill into an EMI (very rare but some banks do provide such a facility on a case-to-case basis), you end up paying much more in the form of processing fees, taxes etc. And in case you want to pre-pay this EMI, you may need to pay pre-payment charges as well.

Also, once you take the EMI route, your credit card limit is automatically reduced by the amount of principal outstanding. As and when you keep paying the EMI, the debt reduces. But till the time you bring this down to zero, be aware of the fact that you may not shop up to the allowed original credit card limit any more. Why? Because the bank has known by this time that the particular person doesn't have the repayment capacity and it is better not to give him any more credit. And the worst part is that all this information is not limited to the bank which issued you the card; it becomes a public information among all the banks and lending institutions. So, in case you go for a home loan after you have converted your credit card bill into an EMI, you may face a tough time getting it sanctioned.

You also need to understand that your credit card is already a loan upon you. It's an unsecured loan with a very high interest rate. Suppose you have five credit cards, each with a credit limit of ₹2 lakh then your CIBIL (Credit Information Bureau [India] Ltd) report will show that you already have ₹10 lakh of loan (though you may not have utilised the limits fully) on your head. And suppose you need to apply for a home loan and the bank calculates your eligibility based on your income to be ₹50 lakh, then it won't give you ₹50 lakh completely. It will deduct ₹10 lakh because as per the bank you can avail of ₹10 lakh anytime using the credit cards you have and it will disburse only ₹40 lakh to you.

Do you carry multiple credit cards? Time to cut them—not one or two but all—and get the records removed from your CIBIL report.

#Myth 12

MYTH	TRUTH
• You should get a credit card to build your credit (CIBIL Score).	• You don't need to borrow money except a home loan and you don't need a credit card for that.

One of the best and probably the most popular myths floated by the banks and other lending institutions is 'build your credit'. Bank, housing finance companies, credit card companies and other lenders have continuously told people for years to 'build your credit' so that when you approach them for any kind of loan, you don't have to face any problem. And how do you build your credit? It is by borrowing money from these lenders and repaying them on time. A wonderful way to sell their products!

The myth 'building your credit' means that to get more debt we need to buy debt. Well, it is a false notion and makes no sense if you want to live a financially blissful life. However, if you want to live a life of credit cards, personal loan and car loan, then you need to build your credit by borrowing and repaying debt in a timely fashion.

As noted author and speaker Dave Ramsey has said, 'Your credit score (also called CIBIL Score in India) is an "I Love Debt" score'. The better score you have, the better you have been in borrowing and repaying your loans. The lower score indicates that you have borrowed money and had difficulty in paying it on time. Whatever the score may be, the underlying fact remains that you have been borrowing money and that is not a very good way to lead a financially blissful life.

CIBIL is not a score that says you are winning with money or that you have a net worth of ₹5 crore or ₹10 crore. Mathematically, it says you love debt and you enjoy making banks and credit card companies rich.

You may argue that if you don't borrow and repay then your CIBIL score would get impacted. And, since in most of the cases you would be availing a home loan, the chances of you getting the loan would come down drastically. It is time to clear some more myths.

First of all, when you quit borrowing money you will not lose your CIBIL score. Rather after sometime, the CIBIL score against your name will show 'NA' or 'NH'. As per the CIBIL, a score of 'NA' or 'NH' is not a bad thing at all. It means one of the following:

- You do not have a credit history or you do not have enough of a credit history to be scored, that is, you are new to the credit system.
- You have not had any credit activity in the last couple of years.
- You have all add-on credit cards (credit card against fixed deposit) and have no credit exposure.

It is also important to note that these scores (NA or NH) are not viewed negatively by a lender.[2]

Second, your CIBIL score is just one of the parameters to get your home loan approved (I don't want you to avail of any other kind of loan except home loan which most of the people will have to take). The lenders use multiple information like your income/salary, income tax return, existing loans etc. to process the loan and having a CIBIL score of 'NA' or 'NH' is not going to impact your home loan approval.

So if you plan to avail of only a home loan then you can easily cut all your credit cards and start living within your means. You don't need to show your love and affinity for the loans to get more loans.

#Myth 13

MYTH	TRUTH
• Credit card allows me to track my expense and keep a record of it.	• A debit card will do the same for you.

This is yet another excuse given by people to justify their love for the credit card. The theoretical advantage of tracking your expenses is that you should be able to bring down your money outgo by cutting down the unnecessary expenses. While most people say that by getting the credit card statement they are able to track their expenses, I have never seen anyone who uses a credit card regularly bringing down their expenses.

The fact is that if you are serious about bringing down your money outgo by tracking your expenses, you wouldn't be using a credit card at the first place. Second, the debit card gives you the same facility of detailed statement (you can check your expenses online using the internet banking and download the statement for your record). However, with a debit card you will not be able to spend beyond your limit and that is a better way of tracking and controlling your expenses.

#Myth 14

MYTH	TRUTH
• Credit card gives me a sense of freedom as it can be used to meet certain emergencies.	• An emergency fund will do all that for you.

Another school of thought made popular by the banks and credit card companies is that a credit card can help you in case of emergency which your debit card can't do. And if you ran short of cash, you can withdraw money from the ATM even if you don't have money in your account.

Technically, banks are correct. But why do you want to lead such a precarious life where you run out of cash and have to resort to a credit card to withdraw money from an automated teller machine (ATM). Probably you don't know the charges that you need to pay if you withdraw cash from ATM using a credit card. It is huge. First, you need to pay transaction charges in the range of 2–3 per cent of the amount withdrawn. Second, you start paying interest in the range of 35–40 per cent right from the day of withdrawal. Usually when you use your credit card at a merchant outlet or for online transactions you get a grace period of forty to fifty days (typically your credit card billing cycle is within this grace period), which is called an interest-free credit period, but that is not applicable for cash withdrawal. When you withdraw cash from credit card, right from the first day you have to pay interest.

And even when you are not withdrawing cash but using your credit card at merchant outlets or for an online transaction at the time of emergency, you are actually tying up your future income towards credit card bill payment; this could have been utilised to a better use such as investments. Remember, your most powerful wealth building tool is your income. And if you tie-up your future income to pay your credit card bills, you will never be able to build wealth.

People who say that they keep a credit card just to meet emergency needs are the people who swipe their cards to purchase new dresses during Diwali and the new year. Diwali is not an emergency; it doesn't sneak upon you. Similarly, new year is also not an emergency. It doesn't appear suddenly. They have a fixed time and arrive every year. Therefore they are not an emergency. So, the justification that credit card is there only for emergency is again a theoretical aspect which doesn't work in reality. In the real world your habit works. And if you get habituated to the access of easy money which a credit card provides, then all your founding principles for getting and using the credit card go for a toss.

The question then is: How do we create an arrangement where we can meet certain urgent and pressing needs? My suggestion would be to build an emergency fund (explained in detail in Chapter 8) equivalent to the limit of your usual credit card. Keep it in liquid form—a fixed deposit would solve the purpose. And don't use this fund for your general expenses. Use it only when you have certain urgent needs to be fulfilled. And then replenish this fund immediately to its original limit so that it can be used later on when such urgent needs arise.

If you are able to create an emergency fund, then first of all, it will give you a sense of security and you will have a better sense of freedom than what you perceive to have by owning a credit card in your wallet. Second, this emergency fund will grow with time as it will keep on earning interest and you will have an enhanced sense of freedom. And third, with the emergency fund at your disposal, you will never fall into a debt trap.

So What are We Up to Now

I know some of you must be finding it difficult to accept whatever we have discussed so far on debts, borrowing and credit cards. I understand that it is very difficult to accept and acknowledge that we have been fooled. Even when we acknowledge it, it is all the more difficult to break the old habit and get ourselves aligned with the habit and lifestyle which is conducive to wealth creation and accumulation.

But the fact that you are reading this book shows that you want to improve your lifestyle and that you want to get out of debt and build a strong net worth. As we discussed earlier, if you want to change things around you then you need to change yourself. This book will just guide you and show you the path but it is you who has to take up the challenge and go through the journey. It may be difficult initially, but not impossible. I too had to face a similar situation when I read, researched and realised how I was killing myself by availing of loans and using credit cards. But, not any more. Today I am as comfortable without any credit card as I was before when I had three credit cards. The only change is that today I am not worried any more about myself falling into a debt trap.

To end this chapter, I just have to say one thing. Credit cards don't bring any income to my wallet. Rather, it's a medium or a channel through which my hard-earned money in my bank account finds a way to go away from me. And if I want my money to stay with me, I would rather stop that channel or better remove it from the system. And once that channel is gone, I am confident that my money will stay with me in my bank account and with time I will become rich. So if you too would like to become financially well off, then stop using credit cards. Destroy them and burn them if you have to. But don't let them find a place in your wallet.

Endnotes

1. In a study conducted by Dun & Bradstreet, it was found that people spend 12-18 per cent more when using credit cards instead of cash, https://www.nerdwallet.com/blog/credit-cards/credit-cards-make-you-spend-more/
2. Credit Score and Loan Basics, https://www.cibil.com/faq/credit-score-and-loan-basics

WATER IT REGULARLY

Chapter 7

Frugality—The New Black

Dr Thomas Stanley and Dr William Danko wrote a wonderful book in the mid-nineties titled *The Millionaire Next Door*, which I think everyone who is serious about getting their finances and overall life in order should read. This book is the culmination of their nearly twenty years of research and study on the lifestyles of America's millionaires.

Remember, if you want to be thin and muscular, you should study the habits of the people who are thin and muscular. Similarly, if you want to be rich, you should study the habits and value systems of the rich. In their study of millionaires, the authors discovered that the habits and value systems of the rich were not what most people assume they are. Usually when we think of millionaires, we think of big houses, fancy cars and really nice clothes. However Dr Stanley discovered something odd. He found that many people who live in expensive homes and drive luxury cars do not actually have too much wealth. He also discovered something more peculiar—many rich people do not even live in upscale neighbourhoods and they don't drive expensive cars.

What the book revealed about the typical millionaires was an eye-opener for many people. While the study was done on American millionaires, the findings are true and applicable for almost all the economies and societies. Most of us have it all wrong when it comes to money and wealth. As Dr Stanley has said, 'Wealth is not the same as income. If you make a good income each year and spend it all, you are not getting wealthier. You are just living high. Wealth is what you accumulate, not what you earn or spend.' The book says that self-made millionaires usually live in middle-class homes, drive a two-year old or older paid-for-car and buy jeans from Walmart. In short, Stanley discovered that the typical millionaires found infinitely more motivation from the goal of financial security than from what friends and relatives thought of them. The need for approval and respect from others based on what they owned was virtually non-existent.

In today's world, it is unfortunate that people judge others by their choice of foods, beverages, suits, watches, cars and other accessories. To them, superior people have excellent tastes in consumer goods. But what they don't realise is that it is easier to purchase stuff that show superiority than to be actually superior in economic achievement.[1] Allocating time and money in the pursuit of looking superior often has a predictable outcome—inferior economic achievement. Remember, there is a difference between looking rich and being rich. And most people in their attempt to look rich forget to become rich.

Consumerism Beyond Means

We, as a society, have grown with the belief that more accessories and better material possessions make us look prosperous. And who doesn't want to look flourishing? We are more concerned with what people think of us than what we actually think of ourselves. Our pride and self-esteem come from the words of praise and appreciation from others, even though they may be fake many a time. And many a time, we too like to fake our prosperity so as to keep up with the Joneses. We too like to impress people assuming they will think highly of us. And how do we fake our prosperity? It is by buying stuff. Just because our neighbours or our colleagues have purchased a brand new car or a high-end watch or upscale furniture, we give in to the peer pressure and end up buying stuff even when we can't afford it or don't need it or when we could have put our money to better use (read investments). And how do we purchase stuff which we can't afford? It is by taking a loan (remember credit card is a loan—an unsecured loan with a very high interest rate of nearly 40 per cent). And why don't we make investments and instead purchase stuff? It is because we don't and can't show our investments to others to let them know how well we are doing in our life but when we purchase stuff, our increased, or rather borrowed, prosperity is visible to others.

The fact is that we like approval and respect from others and to say otherwise is another form of denial. Dale Carnegie, in his bestselling book *How to Win Friends and Influence People,* says that 'the deepest principle in human nature is the craving to be appreciated'. To wish for the admiration of others is normal. The only problem is that this admiration can become addictive like a drug. Today, many of us are hooked on to this drug and the destruction to our wealth and financial well-being caused by this addiction is huge.

Additionally, there is an unwritten rule of maintaining your social status which is congruent with your profession or the kind of job that you do to earn your living. So if you are in the top management of a blue-chip company or an engineer, doctor or a consultant, then you are expected to maintain a certain kind of lifestyle. You need to dress in your best attire, wear the best of the watches in the market and put on the best pair of shoes. And yes, you need to drive a car to match your designation and profile in the company you work for. Otherwise how would people know that you are doing well in your career?

Most of the middle-class and upper-middle-class people spend a significant part of their income just to maintain and display their upper-middle-class lifestyle. Little do they know that rich people rarely care about what other people think and say about their dress, car or house. What the rich actually care about is the work they do, the satisfaction and happiness they derive from it and how much wealth they are able to create and accumulate for themselves and their family.

The third and the most important reason for this consumerism-beyond-the-means lifestyle is the sensationalism on high-end lifestyle created by the popular press and media. We are constantly bombarded with media hype about the so-called millionaire celebrities and athletes and the homes they own or the cars they drive or the vacations they recently enjoyed. It is not uncommon to see headlines about the new car or new home purchased by these celebrities or the recent exotic vacation they experienced. Yes, some of these celebrities are millionaires but they constitute a very small portion of millionaires in our country. Most of the millionaires and billionaires in India and across the world are entrepreneurs, self-employed people or top management officials of blue-chip companies and they have been able to become rich by following a lifestyle of hard work, perseverance, planning and importantly, self-discipline.

However, no newspaper or media will show and broadcast the boring, frugal and disciplined lifestyles of these millionaires. But they do show the lifestyles of a cricketer purchasing an imported car or a movie star owning a chartered plane or a socialite buying a bungalow in a posh locality. The truth is that lavish lifestyle sells TV time and newspapers. All too often young people are indoctrinated with the belief that 'those who have money spend lavishly' and 'if you don't show it, you don't have it'. No wonder, some of the costliest mobile phones and laptops have their biggest market in India and we take pride in flashing the logo of our newly acquired possession. Are we really so hungry of the approval and admiration of other people?

How Do We Become Rich and How Do We Create a Better Life?

Stop Trying to Impress Other People

The best answer to this question is: Stop trying to impress other people. As we discussed earlier, more often than not, we are more concerned with what people think of us than what we actually think of ourselves. In doing so, we keep on trying to impress people by showcasing our prosperity and success. But do we get their approval and start feeling good about ourselves? Sometimes yes, but generally no. Why is it so? It is mainly because other people are probably so busy trying to impress us that they will, at best, not even notice our efforts. At worst, they will resent us for being one up upon them.

Thorstein Veblen, who was a socialist and economist coined the term 'conspicuous consumption' in his book *The Theory of the Leisure Class* first published in 1889. And what does this good sounding term mean? Conspicuous consumption is nothing but spending of money and purchase of goods and services for the specific purpose of displaying one's wealth. This type of consumption was considered to be a product of the developing middle class during the nineteenth and twentieth century in America when they had a higher percentage of disposable income to spend on goods and services that were generally not considered necessary. And a hundred years later, when the middle class has started to develop and have more disposable income in a country like India, the phenomenon continues.

Stuart Chase, who was another American economist, social theorist and writer of the same time period, wrote the Foreword to Veblen's book. He said,

> People above the line of base subsistence, in this age and all earlier ages, do not use the surplus, which society has given them, primarily for useful purposes. They do not seek to expand their own lives, to live more intelligently, understandingly, but to impress other people with the fact that they have a surplus...spending money, time and effort quite uselessly in the pleasurable business of inflating the ego.

Just because the developing middle-class Americans fell prey to this conspicuous consumption, you don't need to fall into the same trap. If you stop trying to impress other people, you will actually kill two birds with one stone. First, your neighbours will feel good about you because you are not trying to impress them. Second, and more importantly, you will save a lot of money which could be used for a more productive purpose.

Live Within Your Means

The second way to become rich and to create a better life is to avoid the lifestyle of the rich when you are not rich. And how do you know you are not rich? It is when you have some or the other kind of loan (home loan, car loan, personal loan, credit card, education loan) which you can't knock off immediately. And in case you are able to knock off all your loans immediately, you need to have sufficient savings (post closure of all loans) which could help you maintain your present lifestyle for the next ten years without working. And only then you could call yourself rich.[2] It really amazes me how some people, who would struggle financially if they didn't get their salaries for the coming few months, live and lead the kind of lifestyle which most of the millionaires can't afford to lead.

What does living 'within your means' really convey? Well, it means to purchase only those things which you can afford easily without availing of unnecessary loans and putting your values first. It means valuing your money which in turn means valuing your time and your life. And it means you care more for yourself and your family and less for what others think and have to say about you.

There are actually two sides to the coin of living beyond your means. The shiny side (which people choose to see) is that you can have everything you want right now. The dark side (which people ignore or forget to see) is that you will pay for it with your life. Buying on credit—from cars to homes to electronic appliances and to vacations—often results in paying two-to-three times the purchase price of the item. However, living within your means suggests that you wait until you have the money before you buy something (with one exception, and that is, a home). This will not only save you the interest charges which you would otherwise be paying to the bank, it will also give you time to decide whether you really need that stuff.

I have learned that the best things in life, including the good stuff and all the materialistic pleasures, come only at the expense of personal discipline. Many of my suggestions may not appear 'fun' in the short run and would look too basic and old-fashioned, but in actuality they are a lot more 'fun' and yield the desired results in the long run. Henry Thoreau once observed, 'Almost any man knows how to earn money, but not one in a million knows how to spend it.'

Understanding Frugality

Oxford dictionary defines frugality as 'the quality of being economical with money or food'. Webster defines it as 'behaviour characterised by or reflecting economy in the use of resources'. In simpler terms, it means that we are to enjoy what we have.

Vicki Robin in her book *Your Money or Your Life* cites an example. She says, 'If you have ten dresses but still feel you have nothing to wear, then you probably are a spendthrift and chances of you accumulating wealth are little. But if you have ten dresses and have enjoyed wearing all of them for years, you are frugal and you have a higher probability to create and accumulate wealth. Waste lies not in the number of possessions but in the failure to enjoy them. Your success at being frugal is measured not by your penny-pinching but by your degree of enjoyment of the material world. To be frugal means to have a high enjoyment-to-stuff ratio. If you get one unit of enjoyment for each material possession, that's frugal. But if you need ten possessions to even begin registering on the joy metre, you're missing the point of being alive.'

Seeing and observing the spending pattern of most of the middle-class people, what I have realised is that all too often, it's not the material things they enjoy as much as what these things symbolise for them—conquest, status, success, sense of achievement etc. And once they've acquired the dream house, the status car or the latest laptop or mobile phone, they rarely stop to enjoy them thoroughly. Instead, they're off and running after the next coveted acquisition.

Most of us have got it wrong when we think that the new material stuff would bring us more pleasure, when the reality is that we derive pleasure in purchasing items and not exactly in using and enjoying them. Too often, I have seen people placing an order for some item online and then waiting eagerly for it to arrive. And as soon as the item is delivered and the box opened, the excitement is over after it's used a couple of times and they start searching for some new pleasure by browsing the e-com portal for yet another toy.

Whenever I advise people on the importance of frugality in wealth creation and accumulation, I have found that they often confuse frugality with being a miser. A miser is someone who is not generous and doesn't like spending money. However, a frugal person is careful and buys only what is necessary. It is not that he doesn't spend money like a miser does. Rather, he spends money on the things he loves or on the things he thinks are necessary and avoids general wastage of either money or anything else because for him enjoyment from the stuff is more important than just purchasing the stuff. And if he doesn't visualise that he would be able to enjoy that stuff fully, he avoids purchasing it. A frugal person is also generous and donates money to charity which is most unlike a miser. In essence, a frugal person makes judicious use of money and that is how he creates wealth. And what is the opposite of frugal? It is wasteful, which is nothing but a lifestyle marked by lavish spending and hyper-consumption.

Remember, being frugal is the cornerstone of wealth building. As Samuel Johnson has observed, 'Without frugality none can be rich, and with it very few would be poor.' If your household generates even a moderately high income (if you are under 30 per cent income-tax bracket then you fall under this category) and both you and your spouse are frugal then you have a solid foundation of becoming rich and wealthy quickly. On the other hand, it is very difficult for a married couple to accumulate wealth if even one of them is a spendthrift. Dr Thomas Stanley, in his book *The Millionaire Next Door* says, 'A household divided in its financial orientation is unlikely to accumulate significant wealth'.

In Simplicity We Succeed

Whenever I advise people on the simple lifestyle that many of the rich and wealthy people live, then one of the questions that I get to hear from them is: 'If that is the way all the rich people live then what is the point of being rich and having no fun?' While it may look obvious that rich people by leading a very simple and minimalistic lifestyle don't enjoy their life, the truth is that they enjoy and live a more meaningful, powerful and purposeful life than most of the middle-class people.

Rich people are in the habit of wealth building and they get much more pleasure from owning substantial amounts of appreciable assets than from displaying a high-consumption lifestyle. For them the real happiness lies in seeing their money grow which will last them for a lifetime. They know that spending doesn't lead to contentment. It only provides pleasure momentarily. And that is why they focus on long-term pleasure and happiness—the happiness of doing the work they enjoy; the happiness of making no payments to bank or credit card companies; the happiness to see their wealth grow; and the happiness of giving it back to the society.

According to a study by Tim Kasser and Kirk Warren Brown,[3] people who've simplified their lives are happier than the mainstreamers. They are less materialistic, less status conscious, more interested in personal growth, friends, family and participating in the life of their community. These people who live below their means have found that there are multiple benefits from rejecting the hyper-consumer culture—less stress, more time and greater happiness.

Remember, your income is the most important tool to become rich and wealthy. However, most people don't use this tool for their benefit and long-term prosperity. Rather they misuse it by spending it frivolously. You should remember that everyone is a victim of Parkinson's Law,[4] which simply states that expenses always rise to match the income. So until you discipline yourself, you will always end up with your expenses matching your income and at the end of the month you will have no savings and you will always be in the same financial state, that is, your net worth will be the same as it was in the previous two years or five years. And when your net worth is not improving, your wealth is not increasing; even though you may have progressed in your professional career from an assistant vice president to a vice president or even to the level of a president, financially you are at the same level as you were when once as an assistant vice president.

You must limit your style of living and you do not need to succumb to the peer pressure, especially the Joneses. You will gain nothing out of the false impression that you try to project to others and the fake approval that you receive from them. However, you will gain substantially if you focus on impressing yourself and your family members by creating a strong and bright future for them. You may, however, say that it is impossible to live within the means. Well, it is not impossible. It may be difficult initially but it is not impossible at all. It will take some time to undo some of the mess you have created, but it is very much possible. The next chapter will help you in this.

Endnotes

1. *The Millionaire Next Door*, Dr Thomas Stanley and Dr William Danko (1998).
2. Dr Stanley in his book, *Millionaire Next Door*, says that most of the rich people accumulated enough wealth so that they can live without working for ten or more years.
3. Are Psychological And Ecological Well-Being Compatible? The Role Of Values, Mindfulness, And Lifestyle, Kirk Warren Brown And Tim Kasser (Springer 2005).
4. Parkinson Law has been explained in detail in my first book *The Richest Engineer*.

Chapter 8

Five Funds Funda

So how do we live a frugal, happy and blissful lifestyle where there is no stress? And how do we learn to live within our means? One of the ways of doing so is through planning and budgeting. I know many of you hate this dirty word—budget—and you've got all the reasons to be unhappy with setting up a budget and leading a boring and dull life where there are no movies and no ice creams. But again this aversion to a budget is mainly because you have been taught all the wrong things about planning and budgeting. However, not any more as we will dispel certain myths surrounding this beautiful yet hated word, budget.

Usually, by budgeting, people think that they need to allocate their income into various expenses—so much for rent/home loan EMI, so much for food, so much for clothes, so much for dining out, so much for health and so much for savings and investments. Most of us, if not all, have tried this method and know that it doesn't really work. Something or the other goes awry during the month and there is no saving; worse there is more of the month left than the money we had allocated and then we resort to the credit card and our budget goes haywire. It is similar to a student who sets up a routine for his studies (mostly during the examination time or when he/she is preparing for some entrance exam)—4 to 5: Maths; 5 to 6: Physics; 6 to 7: Snacks and fun; 7 to 8: Biology. You know how the list goes and one is hardly able to follow it. My advice to the parents out there: Don't suggest to your kids to set up such routines; they don't work.

Another reason for people who have tried budgeting and tend to avoid it few months down the line is that in the name of budgeting they reconcile their expenses on a daily or weekly basis so that they can track every rupee and every paisa they spend. Never do that. It's a very tedious job and requires a lot of effort. And, given the busy schedule of today's working generation, it is almost impossible for them to do it sincerely every day.

And the last reason people avoid following a budget is that they have been bombarded with articles and talks which say that if you follow budgeting and planning, then you have to give up on your desires and stop yourself from enjoying stuff. Well, we earn money not to deprive ourselves but to enjoy life in abundance. And since there is a dissonance between the internal self—your values which might be to have fun and excitement and the external expectation that has been associated with budgeting, a boring and dull life—people avoid budgeting. (Now you must be appreciating why it is more important to live by values than live by materialistic goods.)

Usually most people, including the financial planners, have it backwards. They start from the amount that you would need at the time of retirement; do some mathematics and some backward calculation and then develop intricate budgets that cover everything from weekly fuel expenses, food and entertainment costs to savings for retirement. They will tell you, 'Considering your present lifestyle and the lifestyle you plan to have post your retirement, you need to start saving and investing this amount of money every month; why don't you start a systematic investment plan (SIP) with our bank?' These financial planners have a set of formulas and they just key in the numbers based on your present and expected (future) income and then they hand over the excel sheet to you showing how much you need to put in which plan and how these plans would help you have a comfortable retired life.

Also, these financial planners develop the budget for an individual just as they would for a business entity. And since an individual is not as disciplined as a business entity, the budget is hardly followed to the core as the financial planner had expected. The tens of thousands of rupees that were supposed to be there at the end of the month to buy a mutual fund and to start up a retirement fund have shrunk or vanished completely. And then people complain, 'This damn budget isn't working.'

The mistake people and the financial planner make is in thinking that an individual is similar to a business unit and an identical kind of budget will work for both of them. Well, the reality is something else. The reality is that a business entity only has the budget for its needs. It's in the best interest of the business to limit those needs and cut the expenses as much as possible so as to generate maximum profit for its owner and shareholders. An individual, on the other hand, must budget for both needs and wants. And it is a rare person who can do that successfully because, for too many people, a want becomes a need.

It is human nature to spend our entire disposable income and to rationalise all those expenditures as 'needs'. A business however has no wants. It runs purely on the basis of logic. An individual, however, runs sometimes on logic and mostly on emotion and that is why it becomes difficult for a person to follow a well-documented regimen of spending.

Then how do we create and follow a budget which would help us create and accumulate wealth and at the same time help us fulfil certain desires as we progress financially? The answer lies in the purpose of budgeting. The main purpose of the budget is to save a particular amount of money every month after meeting all your expenses. So why do we need to wait till the end of the month to fulfil the purpose? Why can't we do it at the beginning of the month?

Well, we can very easily do it at the beginning of every month and that is what most of the rich people do. They don't work on the 'Backward-Budget' (starting from the amount that you would need at the time of retirement). Rather, they work on the 'Forward Budget' (which starts with how much money they make now) by following the principle of 'Pay Yourself First'.

The concept of Pay Yourself First was made popular by the great author George Samuel Clason in his book, *The Richest Man in Babylon,* first published in 1926. It simply states that no matter what your present level of income is, invest a minimum of 10 per cent of your net income every month for long-term growth before you make any other payments. This part of your income shouldn't be less than one-tenth of your net income no matter how little you earn. It can be as much as you can but it shouldn't be less than 10 per cent of your net income.

The Richest Man in Babylon offers common sense financial advice through ancient parables and I recommend it to everyone. Over the years, one passage from the book has stayed with me and I have it written in bold letters in my personal diary. And what is that passage? It goes something like this:

> 'A part of all I earn is mine to keep. Say it in the morning when you first arise. Say it at noon. Say it at night. Say it each hour of every day.

Say it to yourself until the words stand out like letters of fire across the sky. Impress yourself with the idea. Fill yourself with the thought. Then take whatever portion seems wise. Let it be not less than one-tenth and lay it by. Arrange your other expenditures to do this if necessary. But lay that portion first'.

Now that we have understood the importance of Forward Budget and beauty of 'Pay Yourself First', how do we start this Forward Budget and how do we pay ourselves first? It is by following what I call 'Five Funds Funda'.

First, open a separate bank account and name it Financial Freedom Account. Put a minimum of 10 per cent of your net income/salary that you receive into this account at the beginning of every month. And when is this beginning? It is the first day of the month. It is not the second day or the third day. It has to be 8 am of the first day of the month when you transfer your take-home salary into this account. And this money should be used only for investment or buying or creating 'passive-income' streams. The job of this account is to build a golden goose that lays golden eggs called passive income. And when do you get to spend this money? Never! This money is never spent—only invested. Eventually, when you retire, you get to spend the income from the fund (in the form of interests and dividends), but never the principal itself. In this way, it always keeps growing and you can never go broke.

Second, open an Emergency Fund Account and put 10 per cent of your net income into this account. The purpose of this fund is to meet certain emergencies like medical expenses, car repair etc. And when do we use this fund? It is when there is a certain urgent requirement which you had not expected to occur.

Remember, the emergency fund is not for buying things or for vacation or for upgrading your lifestyle; it is for emergencies only. Now there are people who don't like the idea of building an emergency fund saying that it's negative thinking and secondly nothing wrong will go with them. And these are the same set of people who carry multiple credit cards on the pretext of using them at the time of emergencies.

Avoiding creating an emergency fund thinking that nothing wrong will happen and that if we stay positive and optimistic, everything will be fine is a false notion. Noted author Dave Ramsey says, 'If you are alive and running around, things will happen to you that you don't think are possible. The only way you can avoid unexpected financial events is by not being alive; in that case they are not "unexpected" events at all. Or are they?'

The basic truth is that you must plan for the unexpected, because it will happen unexpectedly. Although we don't know what form it will take, it will come. Cars do break down, a house needs repair, people do get hurt or fall ill (and you know for sure that with such an increase in the medical and healthcare costs, it has become very difficult to meet them through your regular monthly budget) and you do have to make an unexpected visit to your home town at short notice. To think otherwise is naïve. So you must plan and build this fund. Saving for an emergency fund is an essential part of financial peace and being financially blissful.

One mistake most of the people make in using this emergency fund is to confuse their wishful desires to be an urgent requirement. I am not telling you that you should not try to fulfil your desires. You should do it and there is a separate 'Fun Account' specifically for that purpose (explained later). However, using this emergency fund to purchase new clothes during Diwali or going to a five-star hotel on a new year's eve party is wrong. Diwali is not an emergency. It doesn't sneak upon you unexpectedly. Similarly, a beautiful dining set on sale at a discount of 50 per cent is not an emergency. Remember, your car will need repairs and your kids will outgrow their clothes. These are not emergencies; they are items that belong in your budget. And if you don't budget them, they will feel like emergencies.

And once you have built up a solid emergency fund, you will realise how your dependence on the credit card has come down to zero. Whether the emergency is real or just poor planning, the cycle of dependence on credit cards has to be broken. And a well-planned Forward Budget including 'Sinking Fund Account' and 'Necessity Account' (explained later in this chapter) for anticipated things and an Emergency Fund Account for the truly unexpected ones can end dependence on credit cards.

So where do we park our money for our Emergency Fund Account? My advice to you would be to keep the emergency fund in something that is liquid; which simply means that it should be easy to access. Keeping your emergency fund in the form of stocks and mutual fund is a bad idea because if there is some urgent repair required in your home, then you would be tempted to avail of a loan (use your credit card) rather than cash in your mutual fund because the market may be down at that time and you would want to wait for it to go up (the market is always down whenever there is some urgent need of money). Mutual funds and stocks are good long-term investments, but because of market fluctuations, you are likely to have an emergency when the market is down. So, it is always better to keep emergency fund liquid. But since we need protection for us from ourselves too, it shouldn't be so easily accessible also; otherwise chances of us spending the money would be high. So where exactly should it be parked?

Fixed deposit is what matches both the requirements of the Emergency Fund Account. It is liquid and is not so easily accessible (like the funds in your savings account). Many people would suggest that fixed deposits don't fetch good post-tax returns. Probably, they are missing the purpose of the Emergency

Fund Account. It is not to make your wealth grow but to cover your emergencies. Your wealth building is being taken care of by 'Financial Freedom Account'. This account is more like insurance against rainy days.

Remember, the purpose of the Emergency Fund Account is not to make you rich or to fulfil your desires. The mission statement of the Emergency Fund is to protect you against storms, give you peace of mind and keep the next problem from becoming a debt and that is what it should be used for.

Third, open a Sinking Fund Account and put 10 per cent of your net income into this account. What is this account and what is its purpose? The purpose of this account is to help you purchase big ticket items such as a car, a bike, a refrigerator or a sofa set without availing of any kind of loan for it (we have already taken an oath 'never to use credit card').

Usually, when people purchase such big-ticket items, more often than not, they take a loan for it (when you are swiping your credit card while purchasing your dining table, you are taking a loan for it). But with the Sinking Fund at your disposal you will never have to take any kind of loan and you can have all the material abundance that you desire. Seems great! Good, let's see how it works.

When you get your salary, keep on depositing 10 per cent of your income into this account. This way the account gets funded and over a period of time, say in ten months, it has a good amount of money (equivalent to your one month's salary). And with that amount of money, usually, you can purchase most of the big-ticket household items without taking any kind of loan (if you plan to buy a car then you would need to save for a longer period; until and unless your one-month salary is enough to buy you your dream car). This approach is based on the age-old wisdom of buying something when you have saved for it. Well, it may look like a 1950s method of buying stuff but the fact is that in 1950 nobody lived under the constant stress of paying EMIs.

Another advantage (first being you don't have to take a loan) of using the Sinking Fund concept is that with this you are able to bring down your overall expenses and your savings increase. You may ask: How? Well, let the maths give you the answer. Assume you want to purchase a bike which will cost you ₹1.03 lakh and presently you have savings of ₹20,000. Now you have two options to purchase this bike: First option being the most used; you put down your ₹20,000 and avail of a two-wheeler loan of ₹83,000 at the interest rate of 10 per cent for a tenure of twelve months. So you make the purchase and you start paying EMI for the next twelve months. Let's see how much you actually pay for your bike:

Down payment: ₹20,000

Loan Availed: ₹83,000

Now, EMI for this loan (Amount: ₹83,000, Tenure: 12 months, Interest Rate: 10 per cent) is ₹7297 per month (any standard calculator can give you this figure). So total payment from your side is ₹20,000 plus 12 times ₹7297 (loan is to be repaid in twelve months); which comes to ₹1,07,564.

The second option is to use the concept of Sinking Fund. You put ₹20,000 in a fixed deposit and start putting ₹6500 every month in a recurring deposit. Now over a period of twelve months, you would have accumulated an amount of ₹1.03 lakh (assuming your deposit rate to be 8 per cent). So you go to the showroom put down the cash or swipe your debit card and get your bike to ride. Now let's see how much you actually contributed in this case. Your total contribution is ₹20,000 plus 12 times ₹6500; which comes to ₹98000.

So in this case you made the payment of ₹98,000 and purchased the bike of ₹1.03 lakh. However, when you are availing of a loan you are actually paying an amount of ₹1.07 lakh to purchase the bike of ₹1.03 lakh (the balance amount of ₹4,000 goes to the bank in the form of interest payment). So you are actually saving an amount of ₹9,000 over the purchase of your bike which is nearly 9 per cent of the cost of the bike.

It is simple mathematics. With the Sinking Fund approach, you are able to make the power of compound interest work for you. However, when you are availing of a loan, you let this incredible power work against you.

Some of you here may say that with the Sinking Fund approach, I am not able to get the bike instantly. I need to wait for it. Well, that is what the underlying principle of becoming wealthy is. You need to learn to delay your gratification. Second, once you start putting money into your Sinking Fund Account then usually it will not take that much time (twelve months as discussed in the example) to purchase the bike. What if you have been diligent enough to put 10 per cent of your income every month into this Sinking Fund Account and then one fine day you thought that you need a bike to cruise from Bengaluru to Ooty. You check the Sinking Fund Account and notice that there is sufficient fund to let you make this purchase. So here again you get to buy your favourite bike immediately.

See, it's not very difficult. All you need is to focus and follow this Forward Budget. And you too will find out how easy and effective it is.

Fourth, open a Fun Account and put 10 per cent of your net income into this account at the beginning of this month. You may think that here we are talking about budget and suddenly you brought this 'fun' element into the picture. How is it possible? Well, the purpose of creating a budget is to manage money so that we can create and accumulate wealth and at the same time fulfil some of our desires as we progress financially. And one of the biggest secrets to managing money is to balance it. On one side, you want to save as much money as possible so you can invest it and make more money. On the other side, you need to put another 10 per cent of your income into a 'play' account. Why? Because we are humans and not machines and we need to have a holistic approach towards life.

You cannot affect one part of your life without affecting the others. Some people save, save, save, and while their logical and responsible self is fulfilled, their 'inner spirit' is not. Eventually this 'fun-seeking' spirit side will say, 'I've had enough. I want some attention too,' and sabotage their results. On the other hand, if you spend, spend, spend, not only will you never become rich, but the responsible part of you will eventually create the situation where you don't even enjoy the things you spend your money on, and you'll end up feeling guilty. The guilt will then cause you to unconsciously overspend as a way of expressing your emotions. Although you might feel better temporarily, soon it's back to guilt and shame. It's a vicious cycle, and the only way to prevent it is to learn how to manage your money in a way that works.

Your Fun Account is primarily used to nurture yourself—to do the things you wouldn't normally do. It's for the extra special things like going to a restaurant and ordering a bottle of the finest wine or champagne, or going to an exotic location for the much-awaited vacation or staying in a high-class hotel for an extravagant night of fun and frolic.

And when do you get to spend money from the Fun Account? It is whenever you feel like spending. Hey, I want to go for this party with my friends and I have funds in my Fun Account! So let's go. Or it's been a long time since we visited Goa. Have funds in the Fun Account? Yes. Let's book the ticket.

However, the Fun Account has its own restrictions. Your fun stops the moment the fund in the account becomes zero. So a little element of self-discipline comes in and it is required also to remind us of our long-term goal of wealth creation and accumulation and to live the life of abundance.

Fifth, open a Necessity Account and put the balance 60 per cent of your net income into this fund. The purpose of this account is to meet your regular monthly expenses such as rent/home loan EMI, groceries, fuel, utility bills, tuition fees etc. And when do you get to spend this money? Well, the fund in this account has to be spent all throughout the month. The only thing is that you need to ensure that you don't run out of money in this account while a portion of that month is still there and staring at you. You wouldn't like to look stupid when instead of money left at the end of the month you have a part of the month left at the end of your monthly salary/income.

Name of the fund	**Financial Freedom Account**	**Emergency Fund Account**	**Sinking Fund Account**	**Fun Account**	**Necessity Account**
What Type	Investment Account		Expense Account		
When you put it	First Day of the Month				
How Much of your Net Income	10%	10%	10%	10%	60%
Where to put	Equity, Mutual Fund, PPF	FD, RD	FD, RD	Saving Account	Saving Account
When do you spend it	Never	At the time of emergency	At the time of purchase	Whenever you feel like	Throughout the month

Table: Five Funds Funda

If you observe carefully, you will notice that of the five funds, two, that is, Financial Freedom Account and Emergency Fund Account are for investment purpose and the balance three funds, that is, Sinking Fund Account, Fun Account and Necessity Account are for expense purpose.

Now comes the most difficult part. How do I live on 60 per cent of my income when I am finding it difficult to survive on my full income? Well, if you follow this Forward Budget by applying this Five Funds Funda, you are not living on 60 per cent of your income but on 80 per cent (Sinking Fund Account, Fun Account and Necessity Account are all meant for expenses and the other two, that is, Financial Freedom Account and Emergency Fund Account are for investment). But again, you would say, 'That's fine. But I am already stretched and after making all the fixed expenses, I hardly have anything left. How will I manage in 80 per cent of my income?'

While the question may seem logical and correct, in reality it is an incorrect statement. Most people confuse their fixed expenses to be something which they cannot change and hence harbour the notion that they cannot bring down their overall expenses. After all, how can I bring down my rent or my petrol/electricity bill? Or how can I cut down my grocery expenses and the salary that I pay to my maid/driver? These are fixed expenses and have to be borne. Correct?

Wrong! What people don't realise is that what they call as their fixed expenses are not really fixed but are variable expenses. The so-called 'fixed expenses' vary depending on the person's income/salary and the fact that it varies from person to person means it is nothing but a variable expense. The rent that you pay is a variable expense—you can either move to a bigger house and pay an increased rent or you can move to a smaller house and pay less rent. Your petrol/electricity bill is also a variable expense.

If you find it difficult to manage your overall expenses in 80 per cent of your income, start using public transport instead of taking your car out. And if you have to move to a smaller house, then shift. While practically your so-called fixed expenses (taken care of by the Necessity Account) as well as your variable expenses (taken care of by your Sinking Fund Account and Fun Account) can't be reduced to zero, they can very well be brought down to the level where you can have some amount of savings for yourself and your family.

Remember you have to adjust your lifestyle if you are really serious about creating and accumulating wealth. You need to give up something and that too only for some time if you are eying a bigger and worthy goal. And if you want to create and accumulate wealth, a bit of sacrifice and self-discipline is required from your side. All the rich and successful people have gone through the same phase and if you too want to be like them one day in the near future, then you need to adjust your overall expenses so that they fit within 80 per cent of your income. As Dave Ramsey has said, 'If you will live like no one else, later on you can live like no one else.'

Initially, it may seem difficult, but the fact is that it is doable. With time and a little bit of self-control, it will become easy and you will never realise that you are living with 80 per cent of your income. And with this, you will also learn to live within your means—a major achievement if you plan to create and accumulate wealth and live blissfully.

The second reason why people find it difficult to live within their means (first reason being the notion that fixed expense is fixed and can't be brought down) is that they are neither aware of nor understand Parkinson's Law, which simply states that, 'Expense will always rise in direct proportion to match your income'. So no matter how much effort people put in to increase their income, their expenses also rise in the same proportion and they are unable to save money. With each raise people get every year, their expenses also get a raise and many a times they end up spending even more money thinking that they are now in a better position to afford such goods. So until you discipline yourself and learn to live within 80 per cent of your net income, you will always end up with your expenses matching your income and at the end of the month you will have zero savings to show. But if you follow this Five Funds Funda approach, you will always have savings because that was the first thing you did when you put your money in the Financial Freedom Account and Emergency Fund Account on receiving your salary/income.

Remember, at the end of the day, the question to ask yourself is: Do my expenses, big and small, bring me the thrill they once did? It's not about depriving yourself; it's about adjusting your spending habits to mirror your core values and indulge only in the experiences that truly matter to you. This deliberate and thoughtful spending will allow you to invest in a quality of life that is sustainable and brings you joy. Whether you've got twenty, thirty or forty years to invest, no matter where you are, how much you can save or how many years you've got to do it, you can take advantage of the unparalleled power of compounding when you start putting money into your Financial Freedom Account. Financial security, financial freedom—whatever your goals are, you will get there a whole lot faster when you put your money to work for you. And that will happen when you start living within 80 per cent of your income and invest religiously the balance 20 per cent (or more if you are able to) at the beginning of every month. There is no short cut to creating wealth. It is simple—saving and investing 20 per cent of your income every month. Period.

Executing the Budget

Having understood the concept and importance of the Forward Budget by following the Five Funds Funda approach, now let's see how we execute it.

Some of you might be thinking that it will be difficult to maintain these five funds and we need to have five different bank accounts, managing which will be troublesome. After all, we are used to just our salary account and one or two additional bank accounts.

The reality is you don't have to go to five different banks to open five accounts. Let's assume you have only one account, that is, your savings account into which your salary gets credited and from which you spend money to meet all your expenses. Now what you need to do is go to another bank (not the one in which you have your salary account—there is a reason for it) and open two accounts. Name them Financial Freedom Account and Emergency Fund Account (you can have multiple accounts with the same bank and when you login to the internet banking portal of the bank you get to see the balance of all the accounts and you get to do everything that you are normally able to do with any other bank account). Second, while opening these two accounts, opt for the internet banking facility but don't request for a debit card or a cheque book. Strange it may seem but there is a logic to it.

Your debit card is nothing but a channel through which you get to take out your money from an ATM or spend it while shopping, using the point of sale (POS) machine. Since the purpose of these two accounts is not to spend the money but to let it grow with time, it makes sense not to opt for a debit card. This way you are just protecting yourself from yourself. Since you don't get to take out your money so easily, your money is protected and it will grow with time. Dave Ramsey shares a story of a girl who knew the importance of an Emergency Fund and how she protected the money. He says, 'The girl went to a store and bought a simple glass frame. She then framed it and put $ 1000 in that frame and wrote over it, "In case of emergency, break glass".' Then she hung the emergency fund in her closet behind the coats. She knew it would be safe there and it would be too much trouble for her to get it out of the closet and out of the frame, so she wouldn't use it unless there was an emergency.

So, whether you use a simple bank account or a glass frame, the underlying principle is that you don't use those funds until it is really urgent. You don't have to break the glass to make your routine purchases. But you may think how you will withdraw your money in case of emergency. Well, the fund transfer option using the internet banking facility is always there and in case you need to meet certain emergencies, you can transfer the money from your Emergency Fund Account to your Necessity Account and then use it as per your requirement.

You may also question the need to open separate accounts for saving and investment purpose. I can do that very easily with my Salary Account and that is how I have been doing. Well, more often than not, I have seen people being very carefree with the funds in their Salary Account. Since your salary account is easily accessible and the unconscious thought that runs in your mind is that if I spend the entire money in my Salary Account, it is going to be refilled next month, you will spend it unhesitatingly. This is how people tend to spend the funds in their Salary Account easily. And that is the reason I suggest you open your Financial Freedom Account and Emergency Fund Account in a different bank.

The next step is to go to another bank and open three accounts: Sinking Fund Account, Fun Account and Necessity Account and take a debit card only for your Necessity Account (all your expenses have to be through one account only as this will help you track your expenses if required).

Now you have accounts in three banks.

- Bank A: Salary Account
- Bank B: Financial Freedom Account, Emergency Fund Account
- Bank C: Sinking Fund Account, Fun Account, Necessity Account

Now what do you do with all these accounts? As soon as your salary gets credited, transfer 10 per cent of it to the Financial Freedom Account, 10 per cent to the Emergency Fund Account, 10 per cent to the Sinking Fund Account, 10 per cent to the Fun Account and 60 per cent to the Necessity Account. There has to be no cheating with these numbers and percentages. If you find it difficult to allocate the fund in these proportions then you need to rethink and prioritise. And if you are serious about creating wealth and leading a financially blissful life, you have to follow it to the core.

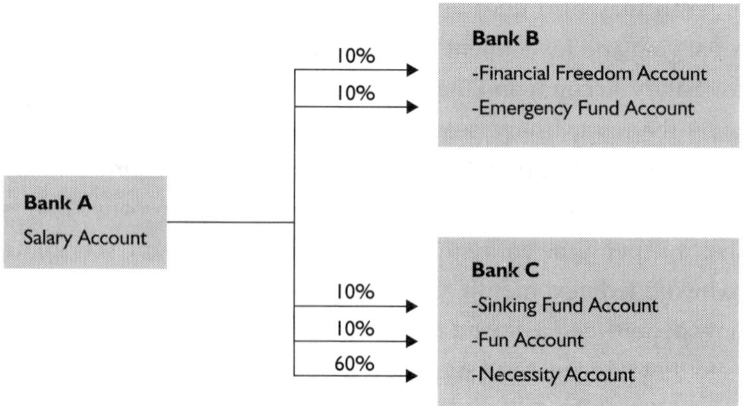

Once you do this at the beginning of the month, you have paid yourself first by contributing 10 per cent of your income towards the Financial Freedom Account and 10 per cent towards the Emergency Fund Account. And by doing this you have set your sail towards abundance and prosperity.

Now you need to manage your monthly expenses using the fund in the Necessity Account. And whenever you feel like spending money on your wishful desires, use the fund in the Fun Account and whenever you want to make a big-ticket purchase, say a refrigerator or a laptop, use the Sinking Fund Account (subject to availability of funds in these accounts to meet your requirement).

Why and how this budget works and what are its advantages over the traditional budget? First of all, with this budget you are saving and investing a portion of your income which you don't get to spend easily. So the primary purpose of budgeting and planning is solved on the first day of the month. Second, this budget doesn't tell you how much to spend on clothes, how much to spend on petrol or how much to spend on food and to track each and every expense. Rather, this budget lets you categorise your expenses into three major groups and gives you the freedom to manage your expenses as per your wish. The only thing is that your expenses cannot and should not exceed 80 per cent of your income. If you think you need to spend heavily on dining out in a particular month, you are free to do it. But you would need to cut down your expenses on other desires during that month because your fun activities are limited to 10 per cent of your income.

Another important point of this Forward Budget—the Five Funds Funda—is that it is not static. Rather, it is dynamic. It changes as you progress in your financial freedom journey. The amount of 10 per cent and 60 per cent as mentioned earlier is when you begin the process. And as the time progresses, you will be able to divert a certain portion from other funds to your Financial Freedom Account. Say, after three to four years, your Emergency Fund is around ₹4 lakh, you don't need to put 10 per cent of your income into this Emergency Fund anymore. You can very well divert that fund into your Financial Freedom Account. Similarly, say after two years of your journey, your Sinking Fund account balance is ₹1 lakh, then again you can divert the amount meant for this fund towards Financial Freedom Account. And in this way, the rate at which your wealth would be increasing would accelerate and you will have more and more money within a shorter time. Remember, your goal is to increase the funds in your Financial Freedom Account, the fund which will truly make you rich. And diverting the funds from other accounts will help you become rich at a faster pace.

Chapter 9

Manage Money—The Couple Way

One of the roadblocks that you come across when you want to create and accumulate wealth is your better half. Now don't get me wrong when I say this. It's not that your spouse doesn't want you to become rich and successful. It's simply that the way your better half deals with money may not be the way you would like to. Similarly, the way you deal with the money may not be the way your spouse likes it. And when there are different forces trying to take the control of the ship, the rudder breaks and the ship is stranded.

Some of the feedback I received from my friends and readers after they read my first book, *The Richest Engineer* led me to think about the need which the present generation feels should be addressed. One of my colleagues said, 'Your book has changed the way I look at money. I am now totally motivated and taking charge of my own finances. The problem is that I can't get my husband to change.' Similarly, another of my friends told me, 'You have presented the financial concepts in a very simple way. I thought my wife, who is from a non-finance background, would benefit a lot from the book. Instead she said, "You're doing a great job with our money and I'm not interested in this stuff."'

It was such feedback which made me realise that I needed to write something on personal finance targeting couples which they could read easily and get the benefit of managing their finances jointly. Working together with my wife in all our financial matters helped me appreciate the fact that a couple's financial plan is a lot like a plane with two engines. If both engines aren't pointed in the same direction or working at roughly an equal power, the plane will have problems. David Bach in his book, *Smart Couples Finish Rich* says, 'Without teamwork, financial planning for most couples becomes a battle, not a victory. And ignoring the problem only makes it worse.'

What Worked Earlier May Not Work Now

Two to three decades ago, when a man was considered the sole breadwinner for the family, he had the maximum say in its financial decisions. Whether it was about savings, investments or any major purchases, it was he who decided how much money should go where and how much money should be spent to purchase new clothes for the upcoming Diwali festival. It was he who decided whether to invest the bonus he had received or whether to purchase a brand new scooter or car for the family. Though many of his purchase decisions, such as buying better clothes for the kids or an automobile, were influenced by the constant persistence of his wife, it was he who decided when the things should be purchased and how much he should shell out to buy those items. The lady of the house, at best, had her say in choosing the colour and design of the stuff to be bought.

Women also let the things go that way since that was the way they had seen their mothers and grandmothers handle the households. Also, money and finance were something they thought should be handled by men. With only one decision maker in the family, with regards to financial matters, the other half silently accepted the decision most of the time.

However, with the growth and improvement in the lifestyle of the middle-class people, coupled with better education, where girls have also started getting the same kind of education, including the professional degrees which were the prerogative of boys alone, things have begun to change. Now the women are no more ignorant of the financial matters and they take an active part in the financial decisions of the family, whether it is purchasing a home, a car, a home appliance or investment. Also, the decision to spend, whether it is on a big-ticket purchase or a small household item—are made by both of them. With the advent of app-based market facility, spending doesn't require paper money or the approval of your better half any more. You just need to place the order as per your wish. And once the item comes to the house and the other half realises that an amount of money has been spent without his/her consent, an argument follows.

The earlier system mostly worked because there was only one king and everybody followed his advice/order, either by agreeing or by surrendering. If he was unwise, it was a completely different story.

Now there is a queen, along with a king, i.e., another power centre—and opinions on financial matters are often divided. This may lead to constant fights between the couple.

The present-day couple can be broadly put into two groups—the first group constituting one earning member and the other taking care of the home and second group where both of them are earning. Now let us see how in the present scenario the average couple in any one group manages their money.

At first glance, the first group may seem to represent the average couple of the nineteen seventies and eighties where usually the husband went out to earn the money and the wife looked after the home. However, in reality, things have changed in the present. Nowadays, the breadwinner spends a considerable amount of his time in office and on commuting as compared to the breadwinner of the seventies who used to finish his office work at 5:00 pm and purchase the daily household items on his way back home.

He has now delegated the job of purchasing and spending to his wife.

Sometimes, a spendthrift wife may purchase new and better toys for the children or other stuff just because her neighbour recently bought the same item. Then a money war is bound to happen at home. The reverse may also be true in case the woman, even though she is a housewife, is careful with money, but has a spendthrift for a husband who spends money frivolously on booze or electronic gadgets.

And this money war spoils the fabric of the family—and with this two things are lost. First, the peace of mind of both the partners, and second their financial freedom, when they should have been sailing through very comfortably.

Let us see how the couple, where both are earning members, manage their money. In this case, you may think that because both of them are working, they would be frugal and judicious in their spending habits. Wrong! In most of the marriages where both partners are earning, they don't really manage their money together. Both of them have different bank accounts (you need to have separate salary accounts where the money flows in). Both have their own credit cards and pay their credit card bills from their own salary account, while the other party, more often than not, is unaware of the expenses. The concept of budget—the Five Funds Funda (either individually or jointly)—is virtually absent and the two meet financially only when they plan to pool their own (separate) monies to purchase some big-ticket items. And when one of them wants to check how much money the other person has been able to save and seeing that the balance doesn't really stand up to his/her expectation, a money fight ensues.

So if you are married and have money fights, you are normal. But if this is a real problem area for you, then there is also an opportunity to improve your relationship and even reach an agreement with your spouse. I am not talking about the agreement brought on by surrender but rather by each one getting a vote, understanding the other's view and finding common goals.

Larry Burkett, a noted author, says, 'Money is either the best or the worst area of communication in our marriages.' And in the present-day busy life, couples don't know how to talk to each other about money. That's because most of the time the husband and the wife have totally different views about everything, including their money. (Well, many don't talk much on other subjects either, but since this is not a book on the relationship between couples, we will stick our discussion to our topic, that is, money and personal finance.)

In every marriage (either a single earner family or a double-earner family), there's usually one boring person (may not be boring in reality, but this is what he/she appears to his/her better half) and the other free-spirited (again, he/she may not be totally free-spirited in reality, but appears so). The boring person is concerned about the future of the family and chalks out plans for expenditure, investment, education for the children and retirement. She/he feels that only she/he is taking care of their loved ones. But the free-spirited one doesn't feel cared for.

He/she feels controlled. He/she feels as if his/her wings are being cut off and there is no fun in working with the numbers the boring person has put across to see what they are going to do in the future. So how do we, the loving and caring couple who do fight sometimes, manage our money so that we are able to create and accumulate wealth?

It is by busting myths. Let's get started.

#Myth 15

MYTH	TRUTH
• If we love each other, we won't fight about money.	• Money has very little to do with love and a lot to do with how much you fight.

If you have been married for some time, say five years and more, you will appreciate the fact that love has nothing to do with money. And if you have just started your nuptial journey then repeat this line for the next thirty days until it gets into your blood: 'Love has nothing to do with money.'

It doesn't matter if you love your spouse more than anything in the world. If the two of you have conflicting values about money and make financial decisions that fail to accommodate each other's feelings about this subject, then you are going to have serious relationship problems. The fact that couples fight over the subject of money stems from one of the following reasons.[1]

- The two of you were probably raised differently when it came to money.
- The two of you probably value money differently and hence spend money differently.

With such differences in your DNA, it is normal. Take a deep breath, exhale and let it go. The subsequent sections will help you overcome this problem.

#Myth 16

MYTH	TRUTH
• If we don't talk about money, everything will work out okay.	• If the two of you don't talk and agree about money, you'll more likely die broke.

If the two of you really want to become rich and wealthy then the first thing you need to do is to be on the same page financially. You need to agree on the budget, the Five Funds Funda. Then both of you need to make yourselves understand that you have to live within 80 per cent of your income and the balance 20 per cent has to go, without fail, towards investments (Financial Freedom Account and Emergency Fund Account) every month. You need to have consensus among yourselves and take pride in the actions that are for the greater good of your family. The two of you need to have shared values and common goals and you need to work together because if you aren't working together, it is almost impossible to win.

Also, it is imperative for you to talk more about money matters. (With due respect, Ladies, in case you are the type who think that money matters are best left to the gentlemen, then you are not doing your part in shouldering the shared responsibility to run the family. And, if you find it difficult to talk to your man regarding money and finances, remember that everything is difficult in the beginning but not impossible. And since you are reading this book, it shows your commitment towards understanding money and with time it won't be as difficult as it seems to you presently.

Gentlemen, if you think women are not intelligent enough to understand money and finances, remember Chanda Kochhar, Arundhati Bhattacharya and Shikha Sharma are/were running some of the biggest banks of the country.)

And when the two of you discuss money and how to manage your finances, then you should learn to listen to the other's point of view as well. The 'boring' person doesn't have to dictate terms to the 'free-spirited' one. Or vice versa. It is important to remember that money is a tool through which we satisfy our wants, needs and desires. When you are chalking out plans to live within 80 per cent of your income, you shouldn't just see that it's your wants, needs and desires that need to be fulfilled. You have to make sure that they are combined with those of your entire family and you are able to fulfil them within the 80 per cent of the family income. If it seems difficult, learn to ration the wants, needs and desires. But no matter what happens, never exceed the 80 per cent threshold because that 20 per cent is the key to your wealth and success and you don't want to lose the key.

Two horses pulling a wagon together can carry a huge load uphill; pulling it in two opposite directions will simply upset the wagon. You need each other. The very differences that attracted you towards each other are still there. You just need to rekindle the charm and team up to win the money game.

#Myth 17

MYTH	TRUTH
• One plus one equals two.	• One plus one equals four.

Yes, you read it right. The reality is that when two people work together to accomplish a goal, they can usually achieve it twice as fast than if both of them were working individually. This is certainly true when it comes to your money. The sooner you start working together, the quicker you can improve your financial picture. Some synergy develops when the two of you come together to achieve something as a team. The only key is to believe truly that wherever you are starting from, no matter how bad or bleak it might look, things can and will get better.

When you work together on your finances, you don't add your efforts, but compound them. No matter what your specific goal happens to be, having a partner working on it with you, providing encouragement and ideas, makes achieving it easier. More specifically, the two of you will probably find it easier to save more money together then either of you will separately.

Another benefit of working together is that you spend time together and get to know the value system of each other—which ultimately helps you develop a deeper relationship. In a nutshell, working together will improve your chances of becoming wealthy and being happier together significantly.

#Myth 18

MYTH	TRUTH
• It is okay if the two of us continue having our separate accounts.	• Opening a joint account is the wisest thing you can do post your marriage.

If both of you are working, then you two will have separate salary accounts. It is alright to have separate accounts, but along with this a merger should begin. Remember the salary account is meant for the inflow of money. It is the account into which your salary gets credited. That's all. The role of the salary account ends here and the role of 'five funds' begins. In an ideal world, you should have a joint account.

If both of you are working and say one of you (A) earns ₹60 and other (B) earns ₹40 then at the beginning of the month transfer ₹10 to Financial Freedom Account, ₹10 to Emergency Fund Account, ₹10 to Sinking Fund Account, ₹10 to Fun Account and ₹60 to Necessity Account. Now you have a Salary Account with zero balance on the second day of the month. Since there is no minimum monthly balance to be maintained in a Salary Account you don't need to worry.

Now the question comes—in whose name the accounts are to be opened. While the first four accounts can be opened in either name with the other person being the nominee, the Necessity Account (the account from which the bulk of the monthly expense has to be incurred) has to be opened as a Joint Account with two debit cards—one for each of you. Both of you become responsible for living within the 80 per cent of your total income. The advantage of the Joint Account is that both of you get to know how much money is left in the account at any point of time. And in case someone gets carried away with the shopping and spending, the other person can gently apply a brake and inform him/her that they need to live within the stipulated 80 per cent of the income for the greater good of the family.

Remember, when you get married you become a team.

When you spend together—achieved though the Joint Necessity Account—it is no more about 'his' money or 'her' money. It becomes 'our' money. We have an income and we have expenses and we have goals. So when you're both in agreement on where the money is going, then you've taken a major step to being on the same page in your marriage, and you will create awesome levels of communication.

Remember, your spouse isn't your roommate. And neither is your marriage a joint venture business. Also, if a spouse has been keeping financial secrets, it's definitely best for them to speak up. It's the only way these problems can be solved. There may be some anger or feeling of betrayal in the partner initially. Nevertheless, a marriage can only improve with unobstructed communication. The key is to share your thoughts with each other, be understanding and supportive.

To conclude this chapter, I would like to quote Larry Burkett who used to say that if two similar people get married, one of them is unnecessary. You and your spouse are different, so celebrate the differences and work together on this money stuff.

Endnotes

1. Spending too much money (or too little) can cause different kinds of emotional pain, Market Watch (November 2017); *Smart Couples Finish Rich*, David Bach (2001).

APPLY FERTILISERS

Chapter 10

Create and Accumulate Wealth

Having come this far, you would have eliminated your debt by now or must be in the process of doing so. Probably, excepting a home loan, you have started living without the burden of paying the credit card bill and have created the Emergency Fund Account. Also, your Sinking Fund Account is sufficiently filled to take care of any big-ticket purchase you are likely to make in the near future. You are now at a crucial juncture. What do you do with the extra money that you have poured into the Emergency Fund Account or the Sinking Fund Account? And how are you filling your Financial Freedom Account?

First of all, pat yourself on the back that you have arrived this far in your journey. You have already covered more than what a very small fraction of the working population has. It is now time to accelerate. It is time to invest.

Wrong Path Leads You to Wrong Places

In my discussion with the people who are well-educated, sincere and hardworking employees, whenever I have asked them about the purpose of their investment, they usually say that they are investing so that they have sufficient funds when they retire.

Most of the financial advisors and planners recommend that people invest so that they can maintain their lifestyle post retirement. The focus is not on helping you become rich so that you enjoy luxuries throughout your life, but to have a comfortable and lukewarm life post retirement. They instil fear in the people that the average life span of humans has increased, thanks to improved medical facilities. And since they might live for a long time after their retirement, they need to have a bigger nest egg or retirement corpus when they hang up their boots. Also, they make you believe that you need to invest so that you don't have to think about money after retiring. The backward calculation starts and you are told to start investing a particular amount every month. Wrong approach to investing, I would say.

There are two reasons why you shouldn't follow the above approach if you really want to become rich. First of all, if you act out of fear, then you do not perform to the best of your potential and the result is not as per your expectation. However, if your action is motivated by inspiration, rather than desperation, you unlock your potential and many times, the result is far better than what you had expected. Then you play to win the game. And when you act out of desperation and fear, you play not to lose the game. And I can tell you that there is a great difference in the results of the two approaches.

When you start investing with the retirement corpus in mind, so that you can enjoy reading the morning newspaper with a cup of tea/coffee later on, you put a ceiling on the wealth you will create in your life. And what is that ceiling? That ceiling is the retirement corpus—the nest egg that your financial advisor has suggested to you once you say goodbye to your formal job.

Secondly, you start playing so as not to lose the game. Also, the fear of not having that nest egg may force you to act and invest in a particular way which may not help you amass wealth and enjoy the luxuries of life in keeping with your talent and potential. You look at your future with fear. 'What if I don't have sufficient funds post-retirement? What if the market crashes at my retirement age? What if I don't get the return as per expectation? And what if I am not able to save and invest as suggested by my financial advisor?'

And with so many 'what ifs' on the path, chances of you hitting one of them are very high. Someone has rightly said that when 'if' and 'when' were planted, 'nothing' grew.

The second flaw in this approach is that you are being trained to think of money as something which is nothing but a 'necessary evil' that must be endured as a part of life. You are told to save and invest so that you don't have to worry about money in the future. Usually, when you give this kind of treatment to the problems and enemies of your life, you try to set up a plan or devise a solution so that you don't have to think and worry about them in the future. And when you treat 'money' in the same way, you don't attract it to your life. You keep it at bay. You want to keep money at a 'safe distance'—'safe' because it is necessary and you will need it and 'distance' because it's evil.

On the other hand, rich people or the people who go on to create and accumulate wealth see money as a great liberator, and with enough of it they are able to purchase peace of mind, at least financially. They see money as a friend, as a tool which has the power to create freedom and opportunity for themselves and their families. Being wealthy gives them the option to live what Ayn Rand called 'an unrestricted existence'[1]. This means having the ability to do what they want, when they want and for as long as they want, without any limitations. It also gives them the freedom to engage in their favourite pastimes, no matter how lavish or seemingly impractical they may appear to others. And lastly, rich people don't make, save and invest money because they wouldn't have to worry about it in the future but because they love having wealth by their side and seeing it grow. And they don't keep 'money' at a safe distance, but close to their mind and heart.

Now why did I point out the flaws in the conventional approach to investment? It is because I don't want you to have just a mediocre life while you are working and then a lukewarm existence post retirement. I want you to become truly wealthy so that you enjoy the luxuries of life not only after retirement but throughout your life. And for that you need to change your approach regarding your investments. Rather than investing out of 'fear', your approach should be to invest out of inspiration—an inspiration to create and accumulate wealth so that you can have 'an unrestricted existence' and help others live the same way. Second, instead of thinking of money as a necessary evil, you should start thinking of it as your friend who will help you anytime and anywhere. You should start loving your money and when you do that, then by the 'Law of Attraction' you start bringing it in your life through known and unknown sources.

Cardinal Principles of Investment

Before you start investing and put your hard-earned money into some financial securities, it is time you are acquainted with and understand the two fundamental principles of investment.

The first principle is to never invest in something you don't understand completely. Would you play the game of chess against a professional without knowing the rules of the game? You will say, 'No'. Then why would you jump into this money game where you will play against professionals without knowing the rules?

Millions of investors worldwide are systematically marketed and sold a set of myths—investment lies—that guide their decision-making. This 'conventional wisdom' is often designed to keep you in the dark—so that you, the retail individual investors, very happily and enthusiastically pass on your money to the professionals out in the market thinking that you are doing something good for yourself while, in reality, you are doing a favour to those who sold you the investment lies.

People lose lakhs of rupees just to prove that they can invest with the sophisticates. I have seen people, completely in debt, living on every credit card possible, just scraping through the months, talk to me about the return of a particular mutual fund or the launch of an initial public offering (IPO) of a particular company. I am amazed at them. How can they think of hoisting the victory flag, sitting in the dungeon? But again, it's not their fault. Our society has made it a sin to make unsophisticated, uncomplicated investments, but it is perfectly fine to have zero savings.

The second principle of investment is to 'Invest Now', if you haven't yet started. In my first book *The Richest Engineer*, I had shown how 'The Butterfly Effect' helps those who start early in their life and how the compounding effect snowballs their little investment into a huge fund if they give it sufficient time to move and grow. We all have learned about the 'compounding interest' formula in our school days but very few of us apply it in our real life. It's now time to revisit it and understand its beauty.

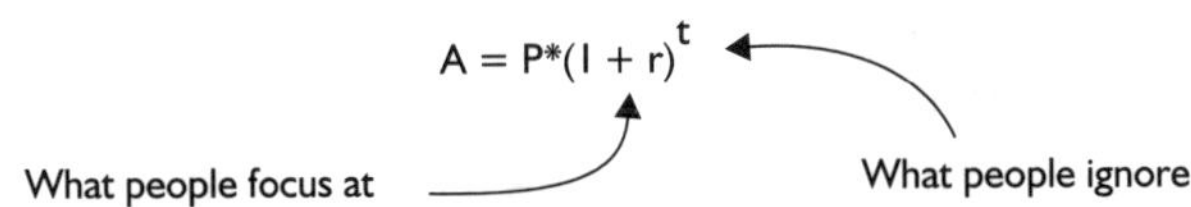

Most of the so-called sophisticates who talk about the rate of return on a particular investment and how they are figuring it out on the hottest stock in the market offering the best return, usually forget the 'time value' associated with the compounding formula. What they don't realise is that mathematically, 'exponent' is much more powerful than 'addition or multiplication'. And if you start early, then this 'time' factor will work in your favour and more often than not, it will offset the lower interest rate (in case it is there) that you would be getting on your investments. Warren Buffett, the legendary investor and one of the richest persons on earth bought his first stock at the age of eleven and he regrets that he didn't start earlier. Now, I am not saying that you too should have started investing at the age of eleven; what I am trying to convey is that you should start investing now and not waste any more time if you haven't started yet.

Burton Malkiel, the noted professor at Princeton University and author of the book, *A Random Walk Down the Wall Street* shares a story of twin brothers William and James, with investment strategies that couldn't have been more different.[2] The story supposes that William and James have just turned sixty-five, the traditional retirement age. William got a jump start on his brother, opening a retirement account at the age of twenty and investing $ 4,000 annually for the next twenty years. At forty, he stopped putting money in the account but left the money to grow in a tax-free environment at the rate of 10 per cent every year.

James didn't start saving for retirement until the ripe old age of forty, just as his brother William stopped making his own contributions. Like his brother, James invested $ 4,000 annually, also with a 10 per cent return, tax free, but he kept at it until he was sixty-five, that is twenty-five years in all. In sum, William, the early starter, invested a total of $ 80,000 ($ 4,000 per year for twenty years at 10 per cent), while James, the late bloomer invested $ 100,000 ($ 4,000 per year for twenty-five years at 10 per cent).

So which brother had more money in his account at the age of retirement? You guessed it right! It was William, the brother who had an early start and stopped saving before his brother had even begun. He ended up with almost $ 2.5 million. And it was James, who had saved all the way until the age of sixty-five, who had less than $ 400,000. That's a gap of over $ 2 million! No wonder Albert Einstein once called 'compounding interest' the most important invention in all of human history.

Tony Robbins, the celebrated author and philanthropist shares the story of Theodore Johnson in his book *Money: Master the Game*. Johnson, whose first job was with the newly formed United Parcel Service (UPS) in 1924, worked hard and made his way up in the company. He never made more than $ 14,000 a year (a small income), but here's the magic formula: He set aside 20 per cent of every pay check he received and every Christmas bonus, and put it into the company stock. He had a number in his head, a percentage of income he believed he needed to save for his family and he was committed to it.

Through stock splits and good old-fashioned patience, Theodore Johnson eventually saw the value of his UPS stock soar to over $ 70 million by the time he was ninety years old.

Pretty incredible, don't you think? And the most incredible part is that he wasn't a high income earning executive. He ran the personnel department. But he understood the power of compounding at such an early age that it made a profound impact on his life and, as it turned out, in the lives of countless others. He had a family to support and monthly expenses to meet, but to Theodore Johnson, no bill in his mailbox was more important than the promise of his future. He always paid his Financial Freedom Fund first.

Now comes the time to regret. If you're thirty-five years old and you suddenly grasp the power of compounding, you'll wish you got started on it at twenty-five. If you're forty-five, you'll wish you were thirty-five. If you're in your sixties or seventies, you'll think back to the pile of money you could have built and saved if only you'd gotten started on all that building and saving when you were in your fifties and sixties. And, so on! It's human nature to have regrets but it does no good to you if you don't learn from your mistakes and take necessary actions.

All those who are into their forties and above and haven't given serious thought to investments, let me tell you something. It is never too late to start something beautiful. George Burns won his first Oscar at eighty. Pranab Mukherjee became the president of India at seventy-seven. Michelangelo painted the ceiling of the Sistine Chapel at sixty-six. And Colonel Sanders never fried any chicken for money until he was sixty-five and now KFC (Kentucky Fried Chicken) is a household name worldwide. It is really never too late to start. The past has gone by. Start where you are, because that is your only option. Regretting has given no benefits to anyone. However, learning from the past mistakes, wiping your tears and acting with full enthusiasm will help you reap benefits.

And, yes, a small note to all of you who are under forty: Don't wait, don't delay; take the help of the 'Time' in your investment journey and 'invest now'. Remember, your earned income will never bridge the gap between where you are and where you really want to be, because earned income can never compare with the power of compounding.

Investment Tools

The following section and the next three chapters are all about investment and how and where to put your money so that your wealth appreciates with time. And, yes, there are quite a few myths to be busted.

Fixed Deposits

Fixed deposits (FDs) or term deposits are by far the safest and easiest way to start your investment journey. It lets your money grow with time and at maturity you get to withdraw the principal amount you deposited, along with the interest accrued during the tenure of the deposit. The advantage with the FD is that the return is guaranteed and your money is safe with the bank. Additionally, you can create an FD using internet banking and withdraw it as per your requirement (if you happen to withdraw before the FD maturity, there is a small amount of penalty that you need to pay to the bank).

However, there are certain constraints with the FDs. First of all, the interest that you earn from the FD is not that great and, secondly, the interest earned from it is fully taxable. So if you are in the 20 per cent or 30 per cent income tax bracket, the net return from the FD is almost at the similar level of the inflation rate and the purchasing power of your money isn't exactly growing with time.

So given the pros and cons of the FDs, the question is whether you should invest in them and if so to what extent?

My answer to the first question is that you should have your money parked in FDs for two reasons. Since it is very easy to open an FD and there are almost no inherent risks (you are almost sure to get your money back along with the interest), it reduces the hesitation to start your investment journey and by investing in FDs you set the tempo of your financial growth and you start getting into the habit of savings and investments. Second, since the banks allow you to withdraw prematurely, though with a small penalty, you can withdraw your money if you have certain exigencies to meet.

Now to what extent should you invest in fixed deposits? Well a lot depends on an individual's appetite for risk. My advice to you would be to invest in FDs to the extent that your 'Emergency Fund Account' and 'Sinking Fund Account' requirement is met. Fixed deposits are an ideal instrument for your Emergency Fund Account as they provide better return than the normal savings account, are locked somewhere in the bank so that you may not very easily spend the money using your debit card, but at the same time provide sufficient liquidity so that whenever a certain urgent requirement arises, you can withdraw it easily. However, don't put your entire savings into an FD, but only enough to meet your 'Emergency Fund Account' requirement as there are better investment tools available for your long-term growth.

Public Provident Fund

Public Provident Fund (PPF as it is commonly known) is one of the simplest long-term investment strategies available for individual investors. Not only are your investments safe in a PPF, they also earn a higher interest rate than the FDs in a bank. Additionally, the interest earned on PPF is not taxable, so you get to keep the entire interest earned on PPF with yourself. And all these factors make PPF an indispensable tool in anyone's portfolio.

However, PPF has its own constraints. First being that you cannot put more than ₹1.50 lakh into your PPF account in one financial year. Second, PPF has a maturity of fifteen years with a minimum lock-in period of five years. Even after the fifth year, your withdrawal from the PPF account cannot exceed 50 per cent of the balance at the end of the fourth year, or the immediate preceding year, whichever is lower.

While many see the long maturity of fifteen years and minimum locking of five years as a demerit of the PPF, I see it as a benefit as it lets my money grow with time and forces me to stay disciplined.

Now consider a scenario where a couple invests ₹1.50 lakh

each year at the beginning of the year into their respective PPF accounts and continue doing so for fifteen years. With the present applicable rate on PPF to be around 8.5 per cent, this investment grows to a whopping amount of ₹92 lakh at the end of fifteen years when the PPF matures. And when you extend it for another five years (you can extend your PPF account in tranches of five years without putting any money into it), you end up with ₹1.38 crore in the account. So, in total you invested ₹45 lakh over the period of fifteen years and you ended up with ₹1.38 crore. And the best part is that this income, including your interest income of ₹93 lakh, is entirely tax free, that is, you don't need to pay any tax on these earnings.

Hence, even if you are not doing any great investments into some stocks or mutual funds, your PPF has the power to make you rich and for this you don't need to follow the stock market or develop some intricate understanding of equities and mutual funds. I am not telling you that you shouldn't invest in stocks and mutual funds (I am a great proponent of investing in the equity market and I will help you with that in the next couple of chapters), but what I am trying to tell you is that a simple investment tool such as the PPF alone can make you rich. All you need to do is be disciplined and invest in your PPF at the beginning of every financial year.

While the maximum amount anyone can invest in PPF is ₹1.50 lakh per year, I would suggest you to fill this bucket once you have Emergency Account filled, before you start venturing into other investment tools. Investments are like driving a car. You need to start slow and steady and before you start accelerating, it is better to have your seat belt wound around you tightly. And PPF is nothing less than a security belt. It gets you into the habit of saving and yields handsome, tax free, compounded returns.

Year	Amount Invested	Interest Earned	Closing Balance
1	3,00,000	25,500	3,25,500
2	3,00,000	53,168	6,78,668
3	3,00,000	83,187	10,61,854
4	3,00,000	1,15,758	14,77,612
5	3,00,000	1,51,097	19,28,709
6	3,00,000	1,89,440	24,18,149
7	3,00,000	2,31,043	29,49,192
8	3,00,000	2,76,181	35,25,373
9	3,00,000	3,25,157	41,50,530
10	3,00,000	3,78,295	48,28,825
11	3,00,000	4,35,950	55,64,775
12	3,00,000	4,98,506	63,63,281
13	3,00,000	5,66,379	72,29,660
14	3,00,000	6,40,021	81,69,681
15	3,00,000	7,19,923	91,89,604
16	0	7,81,116	99,70,720
17	0	8,47,511	1,08,18,231
18	0	9,19,550	1,17,37,781
19	0	9,97,711	1,27,35,492
20	0	10,82,517	1,38,18,009
Total	45,00,000	93,18,009	

Shares and Mutual Funds

This is one topic which requires a little myth busting and hence a full chapter, rather three, detailing the infamous equity market and mutual funds have been provided. And, yes, this is one asset class which has the potential to beat inflation when used prudently. For the time being, let's just hold on.

Real Estate

This is one of the favourite investment tools for most of the Indian investors. We often hear that real estate prices will always go up and you can never go wrong in your real estate investments. Wrong!

Before we discuss the merits and demerits of real estate as an investment tool, it is imperative to bust the myth of real estate investing. You should understand that there is a difference between your personal home—the place where you stay—and apartments, flats, commercial places, etc, you purchase to let out or for capital gains. Your home where you stay is your abode and not an investment. It is just like bread and butter, clothes and cars you 'consume'. Remember '*Roti, Kapda aur Makaan*', the famous phrase which talks about the basic necessities of an individual. Your home is a necessity and you cannot sell it or rent it out to make money. Since you need a roof over your head, your home is an essential part of your existence and you should try to have your own.

So what I would like to cover here are the merits and demerits of investment in real estate which is beyond your personal home.

The first rule for real estate investing is that you should never invest in real estate without having a substantial cash reserve and that too when you have completely paid off the home loan.

I have seen people who have taken loan for their personal home and, once they have cash surplus post their regular EMI payment for the existing home loan, avail of another loan and invest the cash surplus to purchase yet another home (real estate). Never do that.

When you have taken a loan for your personal home and, if you have cash surplus after all your EMI payments, then instead of using that surplus to invest in another real estate, you should try to clear your existing home loan. Why do I say so? It is because you pay too much interest to the bank on your existing loan.

If you are not yet convinced, then try to download the Interest Certificate from your bank's online portal or get one from the branch if it is not available online. And when you see the amount of interest—not the principal but the interest part of the EMI payments—that you are paying to the bank—you will realise why it makes sense to close the home loan as soon as possible. And, if you have been able to generate surplus cash post your regular EMI payment, use it to clear the loan before time. The good thing is that there is no prepayment penalty if you close your home loan before its scheduled closure.

The second rule is that keeping two big loans outstanding at the same time is a bad idea and that is not what I would recommend to anyone.[3]

Most people commit the mistake of taking a loan when investing in real estate, thinking they would take the so-called advantage of leverage. Remember, if you are buying real estate for rental income by availing of a loan, then you should bear in mind that your rental yield (approximately around 3–4 per cent in any metro city in India) will never be able to match up to your bank's lending rate (around 9–11 per cent) and in the end you will realise you have lost your money.

Let us understand this with a simple example. Suppose you purchase an apartment for ₹1 crore by making a down payment of ₹20 lakh and availing of a loan of ₹80 lakh. With an interest rate of 9 per cent p.a. and assuming the loan tenure of twenty years, your EMI comes to around ₹72,000 per month. Now what most people don't realise is that in the initial period, a bulk of your EMI payment goes to the bank in the form of interest and your loan amount doesn't decrease much. For instance, in the first year of your loan repayment, out of ₹72,000 of your EMI, you pay interest to the bank to the extent of ₹60,000 and only ₹12,000 goes towards loan reduction. This, the interest payment of ₹60,000, covers your expense part of the loan and real estate purchase.

Now let us focus on the income part. When you purchase an apartment of ₹1 crore, the rent you can expect from that apartment would be around ₹30,000 per month. So what is happening here is that you pay ₹60,000 to the bank in the form of interest payment and earn ₹30,000 as rent and hence there is a net loss of ₹30,000 for you. And when you consider the factors such as property tax, repair, vacancy and other miscellaneous payments, your loss per month increases.

You may now say, 'What about the appreciation in the value of the property?' True, over a period of time the value of the property increases and you may be able to get some capital gain. But it is better for the investor to understand that selling real estate for an average individual is not an easy task. Real estate is a highly illiquid asset class and if you want to sell your property just because the property prices have increased, then you may not be able to do so easily and you might have to wait for months to sell it. And in that case, you lose a lot of money as your entire ₹1 crore is tied up in that apartment and even if you have to wait for six months, you have lost nearly ₹3–4 lakh in the form of opportunity cost. Not to forget the logistic, brokerage and legal costs that would be involved in selling your property.

Real estate is a legitimate investment tool, but it should come only after you have accumulated lots of cash and you should try to borrow little or nothing against it. Real estate provides some great tax benefits and you can use them to appreciate your wealth considerably. However, remember that you should use it only with your own money, that is, without borrowing money. Because if you borrow, then your benefits come down drastically and in many instances you actually lose money. You can use real estate as an investment tool to your advantage only when you are a seasoned investor, have a very good understanding of the local market and are networked with the right set of people extensively. Remember, your investment should be an asset for you and at no point of time should it turn out to be a liability.

A piece of advice to those who want to make good returns on real estate: Investment in two smaller homes (say ₹50 lakh each) will fetch you better returns than what a single bigger home (say of ₹1 crore) will. So if you have purchased a home of ₹1 crore for your own living and have paid off the entire loan on this home and if you want to invest in real estate to generate passive income, then it is better to invest in a smaller home without taking a loan for it than to go for a bigger purchase and avail of a loan for it.

Derivatives

My father once said to me, 'Never trade in the forward market.' I listened to him carefully, but didn't appreciate it fully until I took my Derivatives class for MBA and subsequently in MFE (Master of Financial Engineering). To avoid the complexities and technicalities of the subject, let me put it in a very simple way. A call option—which is one of the simplest derivatives—is equivalent to a levered position in stock. It means that when you invest in a call option, you are essentially investing in the underlying stock by borrowing money from a bank. So you are basically speculating that the stock price will go up and the return on the stock will be higher than the interest which you will be paying to the bank. Now since we have already learnt why leveraging may not be a good thing to do, it is needless to say that investing in derivatives is not a wise thing to do.

Warren Buffett calls derivatives a weapon of mass destruction and so do other legendary investors. But what did your stockbroker tell you? Well, you don't need to tell me here. You know it and now you know what to do when someone tells you to invest in derivatives. Stay away!

Endnotes

1. *The Fountainhead*, Ayn Rand (1943).
2. This story has been shared by Tony Robbins in his book *Money: Master the Game* (2014).
3. If your main profession is real estate investing and brokerage then you may not follow this particular advice.

Chapter 11

A Good Game—But Only for the Masters

One area in the world of investment which arouses different emotions and feelings among people is the stock market. While few see it as an opportunity to increase their wealth, a vast majority of them view it with suspicion and fear. And they have all the good reasons to do so. I have seen more people losing their money in the stock market than those who have actually made money. And why did they lose their money? Is it because the stock market is a bad place to put your money? Or is it that luck did not favour them? Or is it because they didn't time the market properly in their entry and exit? The answer to all the above questions is a big no.

An average individual investor loses money in the stock market primarily because of his ignorance and, secondly, because he has been taught all the wrong things by his stockbrokers and the so-called market experts who suggest to people to buy and sell certain stocks on prime-time shows. And just like banks and credit card companies, all the mutual fund houses and stockbrokers run their own propaganda—to pass on incomplete and distorted information to retail investors so as to lure them into investing with them. And what has this propaganda led to? Again, a set of myths that have been spread and widely accepted by the people. And once someone says anything against those myths, people are ready to pull out the sword just to prove that they couldn't and haven't been wrong.

However, there is another set of people who understand that mutual fund houses are robbing them of their money and believe that they could earn the same or even better returns on their own.[1] So what do they do? They invest in the stock market directly thinking that they are doing the smart thing as they have spent so much time studying the market. They think that they can pick the right 'hot' stocks which are bound to increase in value in the near future and that they can time their entry and exit in the market to reap capital gains. And do these individuals earn better returns than what the market delivers on a constant and continuous basis? That I would leave to you to guess and I know you have guessed it right.

Just like there are myths surrounding debts and borrowing, there is a bigger set of myths surrounding investments and the equity market in particular. And it is because of these myths that people keep on losing money in the equity market. Just because of their ignorance about the market and following the myths spread by entities with vested interest, some people have lost so much money in the stock market that if you ask them to invest in the equity market, they will think that either you are mad or you think they are. But once again it's not their fault. It's the ignorance and the myths under which they had invested earlier that led them to think of the equity market in that manner. Now it's time to bust them one by one. Sit back, take a deep breath, relax and read the following section with an open mind.

#Myth 19

MYTH	TRUTH
• I can choose the 'right' stock which will make my wealth appreciate over a period of time and this I can do on a continuous basis. After all, I have read books on investments and know the jargons of the market.	• If you do not research stock for a living then you cannot hope to accurately pick the right stocks on a consistent basis. And even when you earn your living researching stocks, there is a very good probability of you picking a 'wrong' stock.

All the people who think that they can do extensive research on some particular companies and then they can pick up just the right stock which will make their wealth grow, must understand that the person who does not research stock for a living cannot hope to pick the right stocks accurately on a consistent basis. Remember, even the normal stockbroker is taught more about selling than analysing stocks which have good earning potential. Mark Twain summed it up well when he said, 'October. This is one of the peculiarly dangerous months to speculate in stocks. The others are July, January, September, April, November, May, March, June, December, August and February.'

Now there would be some of you who wouldn't agree to the fact that an investor cannot pick up the right stock on a consistent basis. Let me tell you about a peculiar game run by the *Wall Street Journal* (*WSJ*) called Dartboard Contest.[2] This contest was inspired by Burton Malkiel's bestselling book, *A Random Walk Down the Wall Street*. In this book, Malkiel, a professor at Princeton University, theorised that 'a blindfolded monkey throwing darts at a newspaper's financial pages could select a portfolio that would do just as well as one carefully selected by experts.'

Since 1988, the *WSJ* has been running this contest where its staff members play the role of the monkeys and pick stocks based on where the dart has fallen and then create a portfolio and put some money into it. Then a set of the professional stockbrokers of the Wall Street pick their own stocks based on their study and assessment and put an equal amount of money into this carefully chosen portfolio. And after a particular period of time, the return from the two portfolios is compared to see who won the contest. And guess who wins the game.

On 7 October 1998, the *WSJ* presented the results of the hundredth dartboard contest. Who won the most contests and by how much? The professionals—the experts of the Wall Street won sixty-one of the 100 contests versus the darts. While it comes as a relief for the 'best' stockbrokers that they won more number of times than they actually lost, it is up to you to think whether you can pick the right stock on a continuous basis. Just answer the question yourself: Do you belong to the elite category of best of the stock analysts and brokers of Wall Street? If not, then the chances of your winning reaching the 50 per cent mark are very high.

The dart board will beat most of us; it beats the best of the professionals too with a 'win' ratio of 39 per cent. We get beaten not because we are dumb, but simply because individual stocks selected without thorough investigation—anything short of full-time work—tend to do poorly on an average. Also there is no guarantee that stocks picked through proper investigation—those picked by stock analysts and fund managers—will do as well as your expectation (remember the best of the professionals lost thirty-nine times against the monkeys). So the notion that you can choose the right stock on a continuous basis is a false notion and the sooner you let go of this belief the better it will be for you.

#Myth 20

MYTH	TRUTH
• The stockbrokers and the market experts have the best interest of mine and they give advice to me for my betterment.	• The stockbrokers and the market experts have the best interest of themselves and they advise you to buy or sell stocks so that they can make money.

Have you ever wondered how your stockbrokers (both offline or online) make their money? It is when you buy or sell certain stocks. From each trade of yours they get a cut. And from where does that cut come? It comes from your pocket. You pay them whenever you trade. Your stockbroker doesn't make money when you simply buy stocks and hold on to them. And that is why I tell people that too much of trading and portfolio turnover adds to their costs, decreases returns and makes their stockbroker rich. Warren Buffett put it very aptly when he added a fourth law to Sir Isaac Newton's three laws of motion: 'For investors as a whole, returns decrease as motion increases.'

There is an inherent conflict of interest between those who work in the investment business and those who invest in stocks and other asset classes. The way to wealth for those in the business—stockbrokers and brokerage houses—is to persuade their clients to act. 'Don't just stand there. Do something.' But the way to wealth for their clients—investors like you and me—in the aggregate is to follow the opposite maxim: 'Don't do anything. Just stand there'[3].

To give you some perspective on how transaction costs can eat up your return, I will quote results from Barber and Odean's study[4] on the performance of individual investors over a long-term horizon. They collected a total sample of about 65,000 investors between 1991 and 1996. The 20 per cent of investors who traded a lot earned an annual net return of trading costs of 11.4 per cent while buy-and-hold investors earned 18.5 per cent net of costs, a significant difference of 7 per cent per year.

A word of caution to the investors who follow the so-called market experts, who predict the future price movements of the stocks, and buy and sell stocks based on their advice: Never take their words on face value. Remember, you just need to have 51 per cent accuracy in your prediction of the stock market to become a billionaire. And if that is not the case then the so-called market experts have been proved wrong more than 50 per cent of the time. And when someone has been proven wrong for more than 50 per cent of the time, they are not really experts. Even an average person can have an accuracy of 50 per cent—it's nothing but 'probability' and the chances of you getting a 'head' when you flip the coin is 50 per cent. So stop following them; they are not experts who can help you pick the 'right' stock.

Also many a time when an investor opens a trading account to invest in the equity market, he/she is bombarded with emails, SMSes and sometimes phone calls on stock recommendation urging him/her to buy a particular stock and sell some other one. The tempo rises when the markets are on the upswing. 'If you don't buy now, you could miss out on a multi-bagger opportunity,' your stockbroker will tell you. However, before you fall for the bait, remember that your broker makes money every time you transact (trade). Your stockbroker is trained more on the salesmanship than on actual stock analysis. His goal is to get you to buy and sell continuously. And when you do so, your transactions' costs go up and actual returns come down. When you are trading it is uncertain whether you will really make money for yourself, but what is certain is that your stockbroker will make money.

#Myth 21

MYTH	TRUTH
• As a value investor, I should always buy low and sell high. And I can exactly do that—buying low and selling high—to make money from the stock market.	• No one can accurately time the market on a continuous basis.

There is another category of people who think that by entering and exiting the market at the 'correct' time, they can make money—and these are the people who keep their eyes, ears and heart on each and every update of the market, ready to buy or sell stocks on some tip or news update. When most renowned investors like Warren Buffett, Peter Lynch, Charles Schwab and many others shy away from market timing commentaries in public, it is hard to imagine that an individual investor with a laptop, a TV running the financial news channel and an online brokerage account can call market tops and bottoms with ease.

People lose money in the stock market not because they 'invest' their money but because they are here to 'trade' and 'speculate'. Easy and quick money is what they are looking for and they think that by being diligent and following the market they can beat it. Let's face it, if there were an easy way to get rich quick, we'd all be rolling in dough. The reality is that getting rich quick is not easy and it doesn't normally happen overnight. Accumulating real wealth takes more than weeks, months or years. It takes decades.

Sadly, a lot of people these days think they can shorten this wealth creation process by actively trading stocks. Impressed by the new technology that allows them to buy and sell securities online—and enticed by the frankly misleading 'come-ons' of some online brokerage firms—hundreds of thousands of people have become what is known as 'day traders'. And what do these day traders do? They simply sit at their computers all day, buying and selling stocks at a frantic pace. They don't make their decisions on the basis of whether they think the underlying companies represent a good investment. On the contrary, they are guided by their sense of which way they believe the market's momentum is pointing. To me, this is pathetic because actively trading in stocks like this is the fastest way, I know, to lose a lot of money.

Day trading is like going to a casino. You might be lucky once and be able to brag to all your friends and colleagues about your win, but ultimately you will go home a loser.

Now the question is: Why can't a person make money by trading stocks? It is simply because you, as a retail investor, have little or no say in dictating the price movement of a particular stock. You should understand that there are very big and powerful players (institutional investors, hedge funds, pension funds, insurance companies) which have the capability to sway the price movement of stocks by playing with the emotions of retail investors like you and me. Second, when you try to trade and make quick money, you should understand that you are playing against the big players who use the high frequency trading (HFT) technique and you simply can't beat them.

To those who are not aware of HFT, let me help you understand what exactly it is and how you as a retail investor (or trader if that is what you do) are at a disadvantage. HFT is an automated trading platform used by large investment banks, hedge funds and institutional investors that utilise powerful computers to transact a large number of orders at extremely high speeds. These HFT platforms allow big traders to execute millions of orders and scan multiple markets and exchanges in a matter of seconds, thus giving the institutions that use the platforms a huge advantage in the open market.

So, when you as an individual trader on your laptop takes, say only a half second to click your mouse and complete your trade order, the big boys with the super computers and complex algorithms in that half second will have bought and sold thousands of shares of the same stock hundreds of times over, making micro-profits with each transaction. Michael Lewis in his bestselling book, *Flash Boys: A Wall Street Revolt*, says, 'The United States stock market, the most iconic market in global capitalism, is rigged...by a combination of the stock exchanges, the big Wall Street banks and high frequency traders. They're able to identify your desire to buy shares in Microsoft and buy them in front of you and sell them back to you at a higher price!'[5]

And, yes, HFT is not only done in a developed market like the USA, it is very much practised in India as well.[6] And did your stockbroker tell you about this? Probably not. Why? Because then you would have stopped trading and they would have lost their commission on every trade that you carried out. Simple.

So when you add the commission that you pay on every trade transaction, the taxes on the capital gain and the odds of your picking/selling the right stock and timing the market, you will realise how foolish it is to trade on stocks. In fact, people who try to time the market end up losing money more often than gaining. Research by investment management firms, academia and actuaries shows that more than 90 per cent of all performance comes from the activity of portfolio design and asset allocation. Individual stock selection by professional fund managers accounts for only 10 per cent of a portfolio's performance.[7] Even more revealing is a study that showed that investors who tried to pick and choose stocks themselves in a market generating a 15 per cent return actually reduced the performance of their own portfolio by 60 per cent, generating a return of just 6 per cent. The study further showed that investors suffer the same fate when they try to time the market.

Do you still think that you can time the market and make quick money? Think again.

#Myth 22

MYTH	TRUTH
• The stock research report gives a true picture of the performance of the company and I can put my money into that company based on its recommendation.	• You can't get a fair and unbiased report.

Banks and brokerage houses regularly come out with reports on stocks—Equity Research Report, Stock Recommendations, etc. Keep in mind that if the financial services industry faces a crunch, the commission rates are on the decline, and most brokerage firms do not make money from this source. The larger slice of their earnings comes from investment banking—the division which helps companies raise capital through public issues of shares and bonds. And a firm (brokerage house publishing stock reports) which wants to get the investment banking mandate from a company will hardly issue a negative report on it.

What should you as an individual investor do in such cases? First of all, never rely completely on a single brokerage house report. Second, do your own research by reading reports of that particular company from other brokerage houses as well. Get a hang of that company by going through its annual report and financials and learn about the sector in which it is operating. It is always better to trust your own judgement than to trust somebody blindly. Third and the best of all, follow the advice presented in the next two chapters.

#Myth 23

MYTH	TRUTH
• Buying stocks on margin is what all the sophisticated investors do and I too should do the same to reap the benefits of investment on margin.	• Buying stocks on margin will make you go broke the moment market turns against your expectation.

Brokerage firms like to make investing as easy as possible for their customers. They have a dedicated team of tele-callers who will help you immediately in case you get stuck in some particular transaction. And if you are new to investing they will also teach you how to navigate their portal and how to buy and sell stocks. Among such other facilities, the brokerage houses also have the provision of providing you money to buy more stock than you have the cash to purchase.

Say, you have ₹5,000 and you would like to invest in a stock with total value of ₹7,000. So what do you do? Go to a bank and take a loan? No. It's too cumbersome. You take a loan of ₹2,000 from your brokerage house and invest ₹7,000 in the stock. As a general rule, your brokerage house will lend you up to 50 per cent of the value of your account in cash or 100 per cent in stock. In other words, if you currently own ₹10,000 worth of stocks, your brokerage firm will probably be happy to let you borrow ₹5,000 in cash or purchase up to another ₹10,000 worth of stocks 'on margin', that is, without your having to put in any additional cash. They'll simply lend you the money to buy the extra stocks.

Why is buying stocks on margin a bad idea? Suppose your favourite stock XYZ is trading at ₹100 per share and you want to buy as many shares as you can because you think at that price XYZ is a steal. Now if you can come up with ₹20,000 in cash, your broker will let you buy 400 shares of XYZ stock with a total value of ₹40,000 by lending you additional ₹20,000. So, instead of 200 shares that you could have bought on your own, you purchased 400 shares. That's definitely a good deal if the stock goes up, because owning more shares means you'll make a lot more money.

But what happens if the stock falls in price? Let's say XYZ suddenly collapses by roughly 50 per cent from ₹100 to ₹50 per share. All of a sudden, your ₹40,000 investment is worth only ₹20,000. From the brokerage's point of view, the ₹20,000 loan it granted you is now a lot riskier. Brokerage firms don't like being in this kind of position. While each firm has its own policy, the general rule is that once the equity-to-margin ratio on your account begins to approach 50 per cent, the brokerage firm will start getting concerned, and you are more than likely to get what is known as a 'margin call'. All of this is stated in your brokerage's margin agreement which, in all likelihood, you would have chosen not to read.

The rules vary from firm to firm, but usually you are given approximately 72 hours to pay off, in cash, enough of your margin debt to lower your equity-to-margin ratio to a level the brokerage firm finds more comfortable. If you can't come up with the money, your brokerage firm will 'sell you out', meaning it will sell off as much as of your XYZ stock as it takes to meet the margin call.

'But wait,' you say. 'I don't want to sell my XYZ stock at ₹50. That's way too cheap. I am a long-term investor. I bought XYZ to hold.'

Well, not on borrowed money. The moment you borrow money from a brokerage firm to finance a stock purchase, you give up control over your account. Brokerage firms have the right to 'sell out' margined positions in all sorts of circumstances, and they do not shy away from exercising their rights. So when your brokerage firm sells your XYZ stock, you suffer a double loss.

First, you lost the money when your stock declined in value. Second, you lost your shares because your brokerage firm sold them to recover their loan. And what was the loss to your brokerage firm? Nothing! They got all their money back. In fact, they made much more profit on commission because you had made a transaction on 400 shares and not 200.

Is your broker urging you to buy stocks on margin so that you grab the next multi-bagger? It's time to find a new brokerage house.

Direct Investing into Stock Market—A Great Place but Only for the Masters

Some of you may be thinking that I am being too negative and conservative on the stockbrokers, the so-called stock experts and the brokerage houses. Well, the truth is I really am as I have seen lots of innocent investors losing their money in the stock market just because they are ignorant of the nuances of the market and how they are lured into the trap on the pretext of some big win. But not any more! I am not here to discourage you from investing in stocks. I want that you should be well informed about the process and know your friends and predators before you start putting your hard-earned money into the market.

Stock market is a great place to invest as your money goes towards the growth of the company and ultimately towards the growth of the economy. Further, investment in stocks should be for long-term. With a minimum hold period of five years, the longer you hold the better the gain. You have to be an investor (and not a trader or speculator) if you really want to benefit from the stock market. Remember, equity is an asset class that rewards you the most if you stay invested for a reasonably long period of time, and is probably the only asset class that has the potential to beat inflation.

But if choosing the 'right' stock on a continuous basis is so difficult, and I really don't know who to trust, then how do I participate in the equity market? The answer is: Do it through the (passively managed) mutual fund[8] route.

As I said earlier, the stock market is a great place where you can put your money for long-term growth but investing directly in the market may burn your fingers initially and you will start believing that it's really a bad place. So as you start your investment journey, it is better to first go through the mutual fund route which invests your money (on your behalf by charging a fee in a number of stocks to reap benefits of diversification) and while you invest in mutual funds, learn more about the stock market by investing a smaller amount of money and see its progress. As you keep learning from your successes and mistakes by directly investing in the stock market, you will understand the intricacies which are not based on any theory but your experience and then slowly you will learn how to reap the maximum benefit.

All the financial wizards and hedge funds managers have done it this way and that is the path you need to follow if you too want to grow your wealth. And what is the path? It is to invest around 90 per cent of the wealth allocated for investment in the equity market in the mutual fund (explained in the next two chapters) and the balance 10 per cent in the stocks which have been picked based on your study and not on tips from others. As you become more and more comfortable with the direct investment in the stock market, you change the mix so as to maximise your return. All the legendary investors, whether be it Warren Buffett or Rakesh Jhunjhunwala, have done it this way. They progressed from investment in mutual funds to stocks and now they own only a handful of stocks. But to reach that stage they have covered a long journey and you need to do the same if you too want to grow your money.

A word of caution to the beginners who are yet to start investing in stocks directly or have just joined the market recently: Invest in stocks with only that much capital which you can afford to lose. And if you are lucky when your initial stock picks turn out to be winners, don't throw in the entire money in search of more such gains.

Endnotes

1. If you are unaware of how the typical mutual fund houses fleece people by way of fees and commission, the next chapter will help you understand their process and method.
2. The Wall Street Journal Dartboard Contest, http://www.investorhome.com/darts.htm
3. *The Little Book of Common Sense Investing*, John Bogle (2007).
4. Brad M Barber and Terrance Odean are professors of finance at University of California, Davis and University of California, Berkley respectively. They have worked a lot on understanding the psychology of individuals in investing and trading. The said study is from one of the numerous research papers that they have published (The Behaviour of Individual Investors).
5. *Flash Boys–A Wall Street Revolt*, Michael Lewis (2014).
6. India is having its own 'Flash Boys' moment, http://www.businessinsider.com/sebi-considering-measures-to-slow-down-hft-2016-7
7. *Smart Couples Finish Rich*, David Bach (2001).
8. Mutual funds are typically of two types—actively managed mutual fund and passively managed mutual fund. We will study and understand about them in the next two chapters.

Chapter 12

Still Not the Best Game to Play

Mutual Funds are by far the best method of investing in the stock market for most people as they take away the problem of picking up stocks by leaving the decision to a professional fund manager. And since you outsource your problematic stock-picking decision to the fund manager, you have to pay them a fee in the form of fund management charges and others.

Further, mutual fund not only allows you to invest a small amount, it also helps you diversify your portfolio with a single investment as your small contribution has been invested in multiple stocks. No wonder it is one the most popular investment tools used by investors.

Now with so many good things about the mutual fund, we can all go gaga and start investing in it if we have not done so already. However, the picture is not entirely rosy with mutual funds either.

Benjamin Graham, the professor of finance at Columbia University and later at UCLA Anderson School of Management, who had taught Warren Buffett 'value investing' and who authored the classic book on investment—*The Intelligent Investor* says, 'Mutual funds aren't perfect; they are *almost* perfect, and that word makes all the difference. And because of their imperfections, most funds underperform in the market, overcharge their investors, create tax headaches and suffer erratic swings in performance.'

So in the following pages, we will see why mutual funds are not entirely perfect and how people lose money when they invest in mutual funds because of these imperfections and their ignorance on the subject. In the next chapter, we will see how we can overcome that imperfection and make our wealth grow. So let's start our journey into the myriad worlds of mutual funds.

Ways of Investing in the Equity Market

When it comes to investing in the equity market, people can usually do so in three ways. The first one is purchasing shares of companies directly as explained in the previous chapter. The second one is to own the shares of the companies through mutual funds, wherein, you give your money to the fund manager and he then pools your money with other people's and purchases shares of different companies, thus, giving you ownership in different companies in proportion to your share of money in the total pool of funds.

Now investing through mutual funds is further divided into two ways. One is the Actively Managed Mutual Fund and the other is Passively Managed Mutual Fund also known as index fund. Usually when people talk and invest in mutual funds, they deal with actively managed mutual funds. So what exactly are actively managed mutual funds and passively managed mutual funds and how do they differ from each other? Before we answer this, let us take a step back and revise our basic understanding of the stock market.

Presently in India, we have around 5,300 companies listed on either of the two biggest stock exchanges, that is, the Bombay Stock Exchange (BSE) and the National Stock Exchange (NSE). So you—as an investor or a fund manager[1]—have the option to purchase shares from this pool of listed companies.

Then there is something called 'Index' which is nothing but a basket or list of stocks. 'BSE Sensex' is an index which comprises the top thirty companies by market capitalisation. Similarly, 'Nifty' is an index which comprises the top fifty companies. And then there are other indices as well such as 'S&P CNX 500' which comprises the top 500 companies and 'S&P BSE 100' comprising the top 100 companies of India. So whenever you hear that Sensex has risen, it simply means that the aggregate value of thirty companies, which are part of the Sensex, has gained in value. Similarly when Nifty falls, it means the aggregate value of fifty companies has dropped in value.

What does an actively managed mutual fund do? It basically tries to pick stocks from the universe of 5,300 companies by analysing securities in an attempt to beat the index. It is constantly churning its portfolio by buying stocks it considers to be 'hot picks' and selling those it thinks are underperforming (also called the 'Momentum Strategy' in the academic and investment community). Accordingly, there are high costs involved in owning an actively managed mutual fund as there are salaries to be paid to security analysts for picking the 'hot stocks', bonuses to be paid to the fund manager whenever they are successful in beating the index and high brokerage and trading costs, as the churn, also called turnaround, is very high.

And what does a passively managed mutual fund—index fund—do? It does nothing. It simply buys all the stocks in the Index without any analysis. So if you invest in a Nifty-50 Index fund, you are basically investing in all the top fifty companies of India. And what are these companies? They are the likes of TCS, SBI, HDFC, Reliance Industries, Infosys and ONGC among others. You get the feel now. All these companies have weathered every storm and have made it to the list based on their performance. Accordingly, the costs of owning an index fund is very minimal as there are no salaries to be paid to 'high quality' stock analysts, no bonuses to be paid to the fund manager as they are not trying to beat the market but simply mimic it, lower brokerage cost and lower trading cost as the index fund managers don't trade stocks but simply buy all the stocks in a particular index and sleep over it.

Now with this understanding in the background, let us venture into the world of mutual funds.

A Sneak Peek into the Mutual Fund Industry[2]

Suppose someone comes to you and makes you an offer: 'Sir, you invest with us by bringing in 100 per cent of your capital and you take 100 per cent of the risk. If it makes money, I will take 50 per cent and more of the upside as my fees. And if it loses money, it is you who lose it and I still get to take a portion as my fees.'

What are the chances of you saying 'yes'?

Nil. Right? You will say, 'It's insane and I am not going to come in.'

But if you are an investor who has invested in mutual funds, then you have already accepted those terms. And who had made you this offer you readily accepted? It was your fund manager to whom you are paying his management fees.

Now don't feel cheated as we, as retail investors, don't have many options or say in how and where we invest our money in the equity market. However, what really saddens me is that people don't really know where and how they are putting in their money and where exactly it is going. They simply know that they have put their money in some 'five-star' rated mutual fund and they silently pray that it will give them some good returns as advertised in its prospectus.

As we said earlier, when it comes to money, ignorance is not good. Now it's time to shoo away the ignorance and bust some myths. All the myths being busted here pertain to actively-managed mutual funds.

#Myth 24

MYTH	TRUTH
• Invest with us. We will beat the market.	• Over a long period, no one can really beat the market except for few unicorns.

There are too many actively managed mutual funds available for the investors to pick. And all are run with the same objective—to beat the market and earn better returns for their investors on a continuous basis. And how many of them have the reputation of beating the market on a continuous basis? Very few—the stress here being 'on continuous basis'.

Even Warren Buffett, known for his incredibly unique ability to find undervalued stocks, says that the average investor should never attempt to pick stocks or time the market. In his 2013 letter to his shareholders, he said, 'The goal of the non-professional should not be to pick winners—neither he nor his "helpers" can do that—but should rather be to own a cross section of businesses that in aggregate are bound to do well. A low-cost S&P 500[3] index fund will achieve this goal.'

Most of us, when we invest with mutual funds, buy into the fund manager's hope that his or her stock-picking abilities will be better than ours. This is a completely natural assumption, since we have insanely busy lives and our picking of stocks would be equivalent to throwing darts. So we hand over our money to a 'five-star'[4] actively managed mutual fund manager who by definition is 'actively' trying to beat the market by being a better stock picker than the other guy. But few people would tell you that 'an incredible 96 per cent of actively managed mutual funds fail to beat the market over any sustained period of time'[5].

Now since the market is the average of all the stocks (including mutual funds which invest in these stocks), there must be some who are doing better than the market and there would be some who are doing worse. And if it is the case then why can't we pick those stocks or mutual funds which will always do better than the market?

It is simply because the mutual fund which has beaten the market this time does not guarantee that it will beat it again. Some of the mutual fund managers certainly have streaks where they do, in fact, beat the market. The question is whether or not they can sustain that advantage over time. John Bogle, the founder of Vanguard and often called the father of index funds, says, 'It all comes down to marketing. It's human nature to strive to be faster, better, smarter than the next guy. And guess what, the other guy is also doing the same. And thus, selling a hot fund is not difficult to do. It sells itself. And when it inevitably turns cold, there will be another hot one ready to serve up.'

But you would say that there are 4 per cent of the fund managers who do beat the market. The reality is that the 4 per cent that do beat the market aren't the same 4 per cent the next time around. John Bogle shares a story. He says, 'If you pack a thousand gorillas into a gymnasium and teach them each to flip a coin, one of them will flip "heads" ten times in a row. Most would call that luck, but when that happens in the fund business we call him a genius!' And what are the odds that it will be the same gorilla who will win the next ten heads continuously?

Even if we assume that you are one of the rarest of the rare investors who have access to the fund manager who does beat the market on a continuous basis (there are some unicorn fund managers who have the reputation of beating the market on a regular basis, if not continuously but again their numbers are few and their doors are mostly closed for retail investors like you and me). But what about the fees they charge? When you actually do the math taking the return, fees and taxes into consideration, you will find that you are no better than the guy who silently invested in the index fund without paying high fees. As David Swensen, the author of *Unconventional Success* and manager of Yale University's more than $ 24 billion endowment fund says, 'When you look at the results on an after-fee, after-tax basis, over reasonably long periods of time, there's almost no chance that you end up beating the index fund.'

#Myth 25

MYTH	TRUTH
• The only cost of owning a mutual fund is expense ratio.	• Expense ratio is just the tip of the iceberg. You pay much more than that.

One of the drawbacks of investing through the mutual fund route is that it entails a cost which is absent when you purchase shares directly from the market. While most of the people know about this, what they don't know is that their actual costs are much higher than what they have been taught to believe.

Whenever I tell someone that he is paying very high fees to the mutual fund houses, he says, 'Hey, I am a seasoned investor.

I look at the "expense ratio" of my mutual funds and it's as low as 1 per cent. Also I have some no-load funds in my portfolio. I don't think I am paying high fees to my fund manager.'

To answer this let me first ask you a question. Have you ever gone to a magic show where the magician performs some tricks and you are amazed at the things he does? You know that practically it's not possible but it is happening right in front of your eyes. How does he do it? It's by misdirection. The magician will bring something bright and flashy and make you focus on that object while they subtly remove your watch and perform the trick. The 'expense ratio' is the same flashy object which you focus on while investing in mutual funds and the fund manager very subtly takes out money from your pocket—and the best part is that you don't even realise that you have been tricked. The 'expense ratio' is the 'sticker price' most commonly reported in the marketing brochure of mutual funds. Yet again, it doesn't show the complete picture.

None of your stockbrokers or mutual fund managers will tell you about the charges and hidden fees. The reality is that in addition to the expense ratio, there are other costs such as transaction cost, cash drag, soft-dollar cost, load cost and redemption fees among others. Hence the idea with which an average investor usually invests in mutual funds—that they pay nothing apart from the expense ratio—is entirely wrong. They pay much more than that and that is the reason they are hardly able to see their wealth appreciate significantly.

In the *Forbes* article titled 'The Real Cost of Owning a Mutual Fund'[6], Ty Bernicke says: 'The average cost of owning a Mutual Fund is 3.17 per cent per year. It is not 2 per cent expense fees as the mutual fund houses want us to believe. It is over 3 per cent and to me it is a huge cost.'

#Myth 26

MYTH	TRUTH
• By giving a 2 per cent management fees to the mutual fund company, I am paying a small price for the service I am getting.	• You are paying more than 50 per cent of your potential return to the mutual fund company by paying the management fees.

I often tell people that they are paying a hefty amount as management fees when they invest with mutual fund companies (actively managed mutual fund). But more often than not, I get to hear, 'But he is doing his duty by choosing the "right" stocks and investing my money and if he is able to give me a return of even 10 per cent annually then giving 2 per cent as the management fees to him is not a big deal.'

Guess what. They have been sold a lie—an investment lie—and they have started believing the myth spread by the mutual fund companies.

First of all no mutual fund can guarantee you a return of 10 per cent year after year (with an investment horizon of more than ten years). Second, assume that this mutual fund has the best fund manager in town and it does deliver a return of 10 per cent year after year. Now let's do the math and see if the small 2 per cent of the management fees is really small.

Suppose beginning at the age of twenty-five, you invest an amount of ₹1 lakh each year and assuming 10 per cent return every year, you would have nearly ₹3.29 crore when you reach the age of sixty. But, if you paid 2.5 per cent in total management fees and other expenses to your fund managers, guess what the balance would be? You may think 10 per cent has made your yearly investments of ₹1 lakh per year to ₹3.29 crore over the thirty-five-year horizon, so 7.5 per cent will make it something in the range of ₹2.7 to ₹2.8 crore. Again, when it comes to compound interest (and costs) over a long period, our mental math doesn't always give the accurate figure. The reality is when you pay 2.5 per cent as fees then your ending account balance would only be just over ₹1.79 crore over the same period.

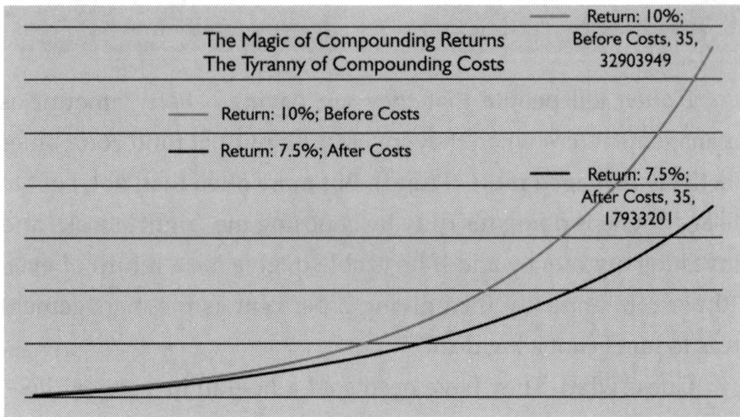

So what is happening here is that you provided all the capital, you took all the risk and you got to keep only ₹1.79 crore. And you gave up nearly ₹1.50 crore to your fund manager. They took 45 per cent of your return.

In the investment field, time doesn't heal all wounds. It makes them worse. Remember, where returns are concerned, time is your friend. But where costs are concerned, time is your enemy.

They say, 'Just 2 per cent is what we are charging and we will give you a return of over more than 10 per cent or 12 per cent.' This fees of 2 to 3 per cent (guaranteed—you have to pay to the mutual fund no matter whether you make money or lose money) when put together with the future uncertain return of 10 per cent may look small. But when compounded over time, it could be the difference between your money lasting your entire life or just enough to make ends meet post retirement.

Do you still think that 2 or 3 per cent fees that you pay to your fund manager is a small amount? Think again.

#Myth 27

MYTH	TRUTH
• I get the return as advertised by the mutual funds in its prospectus.	• You get much less return than what mutual funds advertise in their prospectus.

In the words of John Bogle, this is a grand illusion created by the mutual funds to attract people to come to them and invest their money with them. Most of the people, if not all, look at the past performance of the fund before investing in it. While it is a bad metric to base your fund picking decision on because past performance doesn't guarantee future returns, let us assume for the time being that it is a good factor. So if a fund reports that it has earned a return of 12 per cent net of all its expenses and operating cost over the past five years then it is very natural to think that people who invested in this fund would have earned a return of 12 per cent. The truth is that people wouldn't have earned a return of 12 per cent but much less.

Why? It is because the return as reported by mutual fund companies is time-weighted return and the return which the investors actually get is money-weighted return. You may be wondering what these returns are and how they differ. Well, let me explain it to you with a very simple example.

Suppose you invest ₹100 in a fund which generates a return (net of expenses and operating costs) of 10 per cent in the first year. Your money has increased to ₹110 now. Seeing a good return you invest another ₹100 next year. However, this year the fund returns a loss of 8 per cent which makes your total money to ₹193 at the end of second year. So while you invested a total of ₹200 over the period of two years, the money that is left is ₹193 resulting into a loss of ₹7.

Now let us calculate the time-weighted return.

$$((1+10\%) * (1-8\%) -1) = 1.21\%$$

What is money-weighted return? It is calculated by a formula called Internal Rate of Return which is given by present value of outflows being equal to present value of inflows as shown below:

PV (Outflows) = PV (Inflows)

100 + 100/(1+r) = 193/(1+r)2, where r is the actual return.

Solving it, we get

$$r = -2.35\%$$

This is the real return that you would get. You can't get a positive 1.21 per cent when you have lost the money. It has to be negative 2.35 per cent. But what is the return reported by mutual fund companies? It is 1.21 per cent. So even if you made a loss during your investment period and your money has actually come down, your mutual fund companies will report to you that you have made a positive return. Why? It is because it is following time-weighted return.

Now you may think that it is cheating and how mutual fund companies can do it. The truth is that it is not cheating. It is perfectly legal. The mutual fund companies do mention their method of calculating returns in their prospectus. It is we, the retail investors, who don't read the prospectus and even when some of us do, we are not so financially literate that we understand that we won't get that return in reality.

So next time you hear some mutual fund advertising its return of 15 per cent, ask them what their money-weighted return is. And if you are rejoicing just because your mutual funds are performing well, it's time to get to know your actual return, the money-weighted return, to see how much money you have actually earned, or probably lost.

The Bad News is Over Now

With so many imperfections of the mutual fund industry, now you may be able to appreciate better why your wealth is not actually increasing even when you have been disciplined enough to invest money in your favourite mutual fund, month after month. It is because the system has been designed in such a way that the fruits of all your hard work and discipline are relished by the financial intermediaries—stockbrokers, brokerage houses and fund managers—while you, the actual investor, gets nothing. While you might have been thinking that you are doing a wise thing by investing in mutual funds (actively managed mutual funds to be precise) and not picking stocks on your own and living in an illusion that one day your wealth will increase, the reality is that it isn't going to increase at the rate at what your fund managers may have made you believe. However, all is not lost. As I said in the beginning of the chapter, there is a way to beat the imperfections of the actively managed mutual fund and that there is actually a way to make your money grow with time by investing in the equity market. And what is the way? The answer lies in the following chapter. I am sure you will love the simplicity of this seemingly complicated problem.

Endnotes

1. All the mutual fund houses have fund managers for different funds. It is their job to see where to invest the money that the fund house has received from its investors.
2. Bulk of the information presented in this chapter and the next is based on some of the classic investment books of all time such as *The Intelligent Investor*, Benjamin Graham; *Common Sense on Mutual Funds*, John Bogle; *Money: Master the Game*, Tony Robbins; *The Four Pillars of Investing*, William Bernstein; *One Up on the Wall Street*, Peter Lynch; among others.

3. S&P 500 is to USA equity market what Sensex and Nifty is to Indian equity market.
4. Mutual Funds are rated by various Rating Agencies on a 5 scale level based on their past performance.
5. *Money: Master the Game*, Tony Robbins; *The Little Book of Common Sense Investing*, John Bogle; further, as per SPIVA (S&P Indices Versus Active) report for the Indian equity market, the corresponding figure is between 65 to 70 per cent.
6. The Real Cost of Owning a Mutual Fund, https://www.forbes.com/2011/04/04/real-cost-mutual-fund-taxes-fees-retirement-bernicke.html

Chapter 13

Average is the New Best

As the industrial revolution made its mark across the globe, the town of Sonpur also saw the birth of industries and corporates on its soil. And then there were public issues of shares of these corporations. As the people of Sonpur wanted to be part of growth of the corporates of Sonpur Inc., all the families of Sonpur purchased some shares of each of the corporations. In essence, every family owned some share in all the companies according to their wealth, that is, everyone owned a pie of Sonpur Inc. Definitely, Thakur and Mohan did their bit in the paperwork behind the issuance of shares of these companies through their Investment Banking department which they had recently started.

Each year, people of Sonpur reaped the rewards of investing: All the earnings growth that those hundreds of corporations generated and all the dividends that they distributed. Each family member grew wealthier at the same pace, and all was harmonious. Their investment was growing over the years, creating enormous wealth, because the entire Sonpur town was playing a winner's game.

But after a while, a group of people who called themselves financial analysts and fund managers from a nearby city came to them and said that they could help them earn a larger share than their neighbours. 'How?' asked some of the curious investors. The fund managers then said that they would purchase shares of only those companies which were doing better than the others. They explained their financial knowledge and expertise and convinced some of the people to give them their money and said they would buy only 'good' stocks on their behalf. A manager then handled the transactions and, as a broker, he received a commission for his services. Seeing that people with knowledge of finance were making money, many more such fund managers jumped in and each convinced a different set of investors to invest with them. The ownership of Sonpur Inc. was thus rearranged among the investors with some part being owned indirectly through fund managers.

While in the first year, some set of investors earned a better return than their neighbours, it was a completely different set of investors who earned better than the rest the next year. Further, the wealth of the town began to grow at a slower pace. Why? Because some of the returns were now consumed by the fund managers, and the investor's share of the generous pie that Sonpur Inc. was baking each year—all those dividends paid, all those earnings reinvested in the business—100 per cent at the outset, started to decline.

To make matters worse, while the investors had always paid taxes on their dividends, some of the members were now also paying taxes on the capital gains they realised from their stock-swapping back and forth, further diminishing the total wealth of the town.

People then complained to their respective fund managers about the diminishing returns they were getting. The managers, seeing the result and with a desire to keep their commission income intact, promised to do better next year. So each of them roped in more financial analysts to help them pick the right stock at the right time and exit the underperforming stock and thus increased their trading activity, always on the lookout for better returns. However, this not only increased the operating expenses in the form of salaries to analysts, it also increased the brokerage commission and trading costs. Since all the fund managers were competing against each other to get a bigger share of the same pie so, as the market moved, one manager did better than the other in one year while another manager did better the following year. However, the overall wealth of Sonpur kept on decreasing.

One fine evening all the investors gathered together and took stock of the events that had transpired since some of them made an attempt to outsmart the others. 'How is it,' they asked, 'that our original 100 per cent share of the pie—made up each year of all those dividends and earnings—has dwindled to just 60 per cent?' Their wisest member, a sagacious old uncle, softly responded: 'All that money you've paid to those managers and all those unnecessary extra taxes and trading expense you're paying, come directly out of our total earnings and dividends. Go back to square one, and do so immediately. Get rid of all your brokers. Get rid of all your fund managers. Then our town will again reap 100 per cent of however large a pie that Sonpur Inc. bakes for us, year after year.'

They followed the old uncle's wise advice, returned to their original passive but productive strategy, holding all the stocks of Sonpur Inc., and stood in unison. They no more tried to beat others. They simply grew along with the Sonpur Inc. And this is what an index fund does.[1]

Rise of the Index Fund

You might have got the idea by now about the solution to your problem of stock picking and the many imperfections of the (actively-managed) mutual funds. Yes, the answer is the index fund.

Warren Buffett, the Oracle of Omaha has said that it is simple, but it is not easy. Simple arithmetic suggests, and history confirms, that the winning strategy for investing in stocks is to own the entire nation's publicly held businesses at very low cost. By doing so you are guaranteed to capture almost the entire return that these businesses generate in the form of dividends and earnings. And the best way to implement this strategy is indeed simple: Buy a fund that holds this all-market portfolio and hold it forever.

So what is the fund that holds this all-market portfolio? It is the index fund. Index funds eliminate the risks of picking individual stocks, emphasising certain market sectors, and manager selection. And what remains is the risk of the stock market as a whole. William Bernstein, the author of *The Four Pillars of Investing* says: 'It's bad enough that you have to take stock market risk. Only a fool takes on the additional risk of doing yet more damage by failing to diversify properly with his or her nest eggs. Avoid the problem—buy a well-run index fund and own the whole market.'

So what happens when you invest in a passively managed mutual fund which tracks Nifty 50? You basically own a piece of all the top fifty companies which are present in the Nifty Index. Remember these are the top tier companies which have shown incredible resilience. The average investor calls them blue chip companies.

And what are the benefits of investing in an index fund? Well, there are multiple benefits:

- *Low Cost of Investment*: With an index fund you don't have to pay a professional to try picking stocks in the index you want to own. It's effectively been done for you by the market and the fund manager just has to pick the stocks already there on the list. It's a no-brainer and that is the reason management fees of an index fund can be as low as 0.3 to 0.5% as against the fees of nearly 2.5 to 3 per cent for actively managed funds.

- *Low Transaction and Trading Cost:* Since these funds are not actively managed, that is, they do not buy and sell stocks to generate extra returns, they incur lower transaction costs than actively managed funds. Hence there are low trading and brokerage costs.
- *Lower Tax Liability*[2]: Third, since index funds don't convert your notional profit into real profit by buying and selling shares at the level actively-managed mutual funds do, the investors pay lower taxes to the government and their overall wealth increases at a more rapid rate.
- *Peace of Mind*: The best part of owning an index fund is that you don't have to keep track of your fund's performance. You don't have to think whether your fund is beating the market or getting beaten by the market. You are assured of your fund growth as long as the total economy of India is doing well.

As John Bogle says, 'Index funds operate with minimal expenses and with no advisory fees, with a tiny portfolio turnover, and with high tax efficiency.'

When an investor tries to beat the market by investing in an actively managed mutual fund in the hope that his fund manager will pick the best stocks, sometimes he may win and sometimes he may lose. And whenever he wins, there would be a corresponding loser on the other side of the trade and whenever he loses there would be some winner. So you may think that on an average, trading is a zero-sum game. Well, the reality is not what everyone has been taught to believe. The reality is that in every trade, the gains made by one party are always less than the loss made by the other party. Why? It is because a portion from the transaction has been consumed by the stockbroker and the fund manager in the form of various fees.

So when we subtract those costs of financial intermediaries—all those management fees, all that portfolio turnover, all of those brokerage commissions, all of those sales loads, all of those advertising costs, all of those operating costs, all of those legal fees—the returns of investors as a group must, will and does fall short of the market return by an amount precisely equal to the aggregate amount of those costs. This is a simple and harsh fact of investing when you invest with actively managed mutual funds.

So when India Inc. offers a return of 10 per cent, the investors don't get that return. What remains with them after they pay their financial intermediaries is 7 to 7.5 per cent. The worst part is investors pay their intermediaries no matter whether the return is positive, zero or even negative. Hence the reality is that before costs, beating the market is a zero sum game but after costs, it is a loser's game. As Warren Buffett[3] recently wrote, 'When trillions of dollars are managed by Wall Streeters charging high fees, it will usually be the managers who reap outsize profits, not the clients.'

In the casino, it is the casino owner who always wins. In horse racing, the track always wins. In any lottery, the state always wins. Similarly in the game of investing, when one tries to beat the other, the fund managers and the financial brokers always win and investors lose as a group. Successful investing is then all about minimising the portion of returns earned by India Inc, that is consumed by Dalal Street, and maximising the share of returns that is delivered to the main street. And who lives on the main street? It is investors like you and me. So simply buy a Nifty 500 or S&P BSE 500 Index Fund. Then, once you have bought your stocks, get out of the casino and stay out. Just hold the market portfolio forever and watch your wealth grow as India Inc. grows year after year.

Burton Malkiel, author of *A Random Walk Down the Wall Street* and Princeton University professor once said, 'Index funds have regularly produced annual rates of return exceeding those of active managers by close of 2 percentage points. Active management as a whole cannot achieve gross returns exceeding the market as a whole, and therefore they must, on an average, underperform the indexes by the amount of these expenses and transaction cost.'

Investing in index funds is very similar to what Lord Hanuman did when he was asked to bring the *Sanjeevini-booti* (a medicinal herb) from the Kailash mountain. Confused between similar looking herbs, Lord Hanuman did what was the best. He picked the entire mountain knowing that if he brought the mountain, he would be carrying the *Sanjeevini-booti* too. While in the case of Lord Hanuman it was difficult to carry the heavy mountain and only someone with his mighty strength could have carried it on his shoulder, in our case carrying the mountain is rather easy and less expensive. We just need to invest in the entire stock market at a very low cost and with this we are assured of the return that the market would give us.

Remember, you don't have to waste your time trying to pick stocks yourself or the best mutual fund available in the market. A portfolio of low-cost index funds is the best approach for a percentage of your investments because we don't know what stocks will be the 'best' going forward. And how cool is it to know that by 'passively' owning the market, you are beating 96 per cent of the world's 'expert' mutual fund managers and nearly as many hedge fund managers. It's time to free yourself from the burden of trying to pick the winner of the race. John Bogle once said, 'In investing it feels counterintuitive. The secret is don't do anything; just stand there!' And by becoming the market and not trying to beat it, you are on the side of progress, growth and expansion.

Benjamin Graham, however, says that the index funds have

one significant flaw: They are boring. You'll never be able to go to a club and brag about how you own the top-performing fund in the market. You'll never be able to boast that you beat the market, because the job of an index fund is to match the market's return and not to exceed it. Your index fund manager is not likely to roll the dice at a casino and gamble that the next great industry will be textile or technology. Your index fund will always own every stock, not just one manager's best guess at the next new thing. You may not see the true benefit of index fund over the actively managed funds in the first few years but as the years pass, the cost advantage of indexing will keep accruing relentlessly. Hold an index fund for fifteen years or more, adding money every month, and you are all but certain to outperform the vast majority of professional and individual investors alike.[4]

Index Funds Serve the Purpose of Investment

While index funds have multiple benefits which have been discussed by professionals and academicians alike in various literature, it has one special benefit which not many people have discussed so far. And what is that benefit? Well the benefit is that it is the index fund which beats inflation on a consistent basis.

Now let's understand how an index fund does it. One of the primary objectives of investment is to beat inflation so that effective purchasing power of your money doesn't go down with time. Ever wondered what happens with inflation? In simple terms, inflation means that the cost of the goods that you purchase and consume increases every year. So with inflation, the price of wheat flour, rice, toothpaste, cement and clothes etc. increases every year and you feel a pinch in your pocket whenever you have to pay a higher price for salt or oil. And where does this increased money from your pocket go? It goes to the company and ultimately to the shareholders of that company which manufactures those products. And what will happen if you are one of the shareholders of those companies? Your monies come back to your own pocket. So, if we own a little piece of those companies that make those products, we are virtually guaranteed to stay ahead of inflation and we get a little of the money back which those companies have been getting off us for years.

And guess what, index funds help us achieve this. When you invest in an index fund that purchases shares in the top 500 companies of India, you virtually own a share of stocks in companies that make everything from tyres to toothpastes, flour to processed food and cement to coke. This is one area where index funds score over direct investing into stocks and actively-managed mutual funds because it is practically impossible (and not advisable also) for an individual investor to hold so many stocks.

Is Index Fund Good for India?

Now some of you who have been investing in the equity market for some time wouldn't agree. You would say that investment in a low-cost index fund may be good for a developed economy like the USA but in developing economy like India, where the market is not fully efficient, developed and mature, the actively managed mutual fund still rules the roost—generating alphas[5] for their investors.

Well it is true that because of information asymmetry and lack of proper regulatory control over the market, there is still some scope for active fund managers to beat the market, but with the improvement in the technology and gradual decrease in the information asymmetry, the difference in the return between an actively managed mutual fund and a passively managed mutual fund has been decreasing and it is just a matter of time when the average return of the actively managed mutual fund (net of management fees and taxes) will match that of an index fund in India as well.

SK Lokeshwari, the associate editor and head of research at

The Hindu Business Line wrote an article titled 'An Active Ride the Passive Way'[6] in April 2017. In this article he says that the difference between the return of actively managed large-cap funds and the index funds has narrowed considerably in recent times in India. For instance, in the bull market from March 2003 to December 2007, large-cap funds were able to deliver average returns that were 12 percentage points higher than index funds, when one-year rolling returns of both categories were considered. And when markets recovered from the 2008 crash, the average daily performance of large-cap funds was 6.5 percentage points higher in the period between March 2009 and October 2010. However, if we consider the recent phases of market up-cycles, from September 2013 to January 2015 or from February 2016 to mid-2018, the out-performance gap has narrowed considerably to 2.7 and 1.8 percentage points, respectively.

Second, even if we assume that stock market in India is still not as efficient[7] as that of the other developed countries and an actively managed mutual fund still has some scope of delivering better returns, the mathematics however tells a different story. Whether markets are efficient or inefficient, all investors as a group must earn the return the stock market delivers. And if in an inefficient market, the most successful fund managers achieve some unusually higher returns, then there would be some other active fund managers who would have suffered unusually higher losses, because if someone has done better than average then there would be someone who has done less too. So, the notion that actively managed mutual fund does better than index fund in India is nothing more than a marketing gimmick spread by all the active mutual fund companies so that they continue to earn fees and commissions from their investors.

Third, as we have seen earlier that while there are actively managed funds which do beat the market, the chances of the same fund beating the market the next time are very low. In this case, investing in actively managed mutual fund is very similar to purchasing the shares of the companies directly. While in the case of shares you rely on your judgement to pick the right stock, in the case of an actively managed mutual fund you have to rely on your judgement to pick the right fund. And the result is often that your net return (after all the fees and cost) is lower than what the market delivers.

Fourth, people say that index funds in India invest in only a small number of companies—thirty to fifty companies—which are mostly large-cap stocks with a lower possibility of high growth and leave out a large number of mid-cap and small-cap stocks which have a good potential to grow. True. But again it's not their fault. It's their ignorance which makes them think so. The reality is that there are indices which cover a large number of companies such as S&P CNX 500, Nifty 500 and S&P BSE 500 to name a few. So when you have invested in Nifty 500, you basically cover 95.2 per cent[8] of the total free-float market of the stock. And when you have invested in over 95 per cent of the total stock market, you have actually invested in the entire market.

Not All Guarantees are Good

Assuming that you have gained insights into the equity market and mutual fund industry, you become an equity investor and invest your money in the stock market by buying an index fund. One fine day when you read the morning newspaper and find that the stock market has dropped and consequently the value of your fund has plummeted, you wonder, 'Is my money safe?'

Before I answer your question let me tell you something about Sir John Templeton, a British investor, fund manager and philanthropist. Templeton came from humble beginnings in Tennessee. He had to drop out of college because he couldn't afford the tuition but, even as a young man, he recognised the incremental power of compounded savings. He committed to setting aside 50 per cent of what he earned, and then he took his savings and put them to work in a big way. So when Germany was invading Poland in 1939, plunging Europe into World War II and paralysing the world with fear and despair, he scraped together $ 10,000 to invest in the New York stock market. He bought 100 shares of every company trading under $ 1, including those considered nearly bankrupt. But he knew what so many people forget that night is not forever. Financial winter is a season and it's followed by spring.

After World War II ended in 1945, the US economy surged and Templeton's shares exploded into a multibillion-dollar portfolio.[9] We saw the same kind of growth happen as the stock market soared from the lows of 2008–09 (see the following graph of BSE over the past twenty years), but most people missed this surge post the 2008–09 debacle. Why? Because when things are going down, we think they're going to stay down forever and pessimism takes over. However, those who have understood the equity market well and have the foresight of Sir Templeton will make huge profits.

Even if you see how the Sensex or Nifty have done on an average over a period of ten or twenty years, you will realise that both of them have seen an upward trend with troughs and crests in between.

When asked what keeps most individual investors from succeeding in the stock market, Benjamin Graham said, 'The primary cause of failure is that they pay too much attention to what the stock market is doing currently.'

The market does come down for some period and it may come down further. And it is at this time that individual investors are tested for their patience, trust in the company and the overall economy. Remember, the market goes up and down all the time. And since the market moves more on the people's emotions—fear and greed—than on the logic, sometimes its movement can be pretty wild.

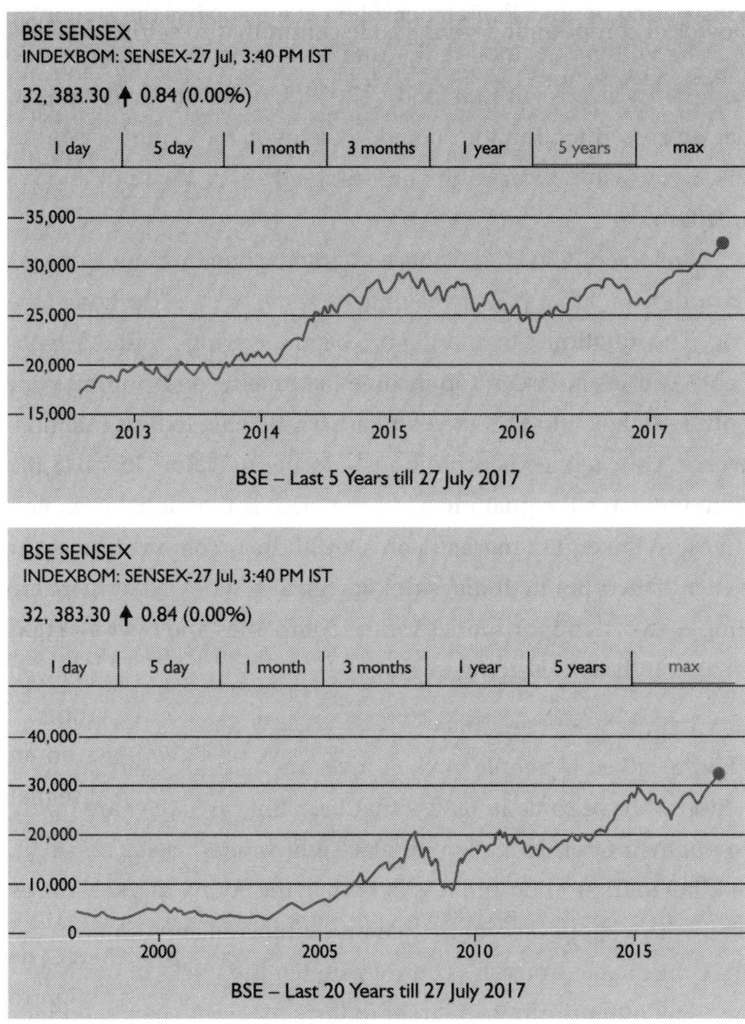

Source: BSE, Date 27 July 2017

You can't expect a guaranteed return in the equity market and that is the real beauty of it. A guaranteed income limits the level to which one can earn. But when you participate in the market and flow along with it and not try to beat it, you are bound to get a good return; the only thing is that you have to stay put for a long period of time. Remember, a lion at the zoo has the guarantee that he will get his food daily (unlike the lion in the jungle who sometimes sleeps without food). The king of the jungle is made to eat processed food in the zoo and when you look into his soulful eyes, you will notice that he misses the thrill of the hunt and his freedom.[10]

Anyone of you who wants a guarantee on your money needs to understand that you are paying the same price as the lion in the zoo. The inflation rate in India has been hovering around 5–6 per cent. And if you are in top income tax bracket and putting your entire savings into FDs then you are barely able to beat inflation; worse, your money is continuously losing its value. Just like the lion, you have the guarantee but the price is too high. When you invest in the equity market, you should draw comfort from your belief that corporate India is doing well as a whole, that there are ample growth opportunities for the companies and over a period of time India Inc. is going to grow.

Control the Controllable

Having talked to people on their investments and observing their actions, I have come to realise that in many cases they are trying to put their effort in the wrong place which often yields no result, leading to frustration and loss of faith in the equity market. You as an investor should recognise that investing is all about controlling the controllable. You can't control whether the stocks or funds you buy will outperform the market today, next week, next month or next year. You can't control the various macroeconomic factors which affect the entire equity market, nor can you control the sector-specific factors which affect the sectors in which you have invested. If you try to do any of these, basically you will be barking up the wrong tree. However, you can control[11]:

- *Your brokerage cost*: By trading rarely, patiently and cheaply

- *Your ownership cost*: By refusing to buy mutual funds with excessive annual expenses
- *Your expectations*: By using reality, not fantasy, to forecast your returns
- *Your risk*: By deciding how many of your total assets to put at hazard in the stock market, by diversifying and by re-balancing
- *Your taxes*: By holding stocks and funds for at least a year and, whenever possible, for at least five years, to lower your capital gains tax
- And most of all, your own behaviour

Investing isn't about beating others at their game. It's about controlling yourself at your own game. The challenge for the intelligent investor is not to find the stocks that will go up the most and down the least, but rather to prevent him from being his own worst enemy—from buying much just because the market says 'buy' and from selling just because market says 'sell'.

If your investment horizon is long, and that is what it should be, for at least fifteen to twenty years, there is only one sensible approach: Buy every month, automatically and whenever else you can spare some money. And the single best choice for this lifelong holding is a total stock market index fund. And when do you sell it? Never, until and unless you are in dire need of cash.

Investing Isn't So Hard

Learning to invest is like learning a foreign language. Initially it may seem to be a daunting task but, as you progress in your investment journey, it won't be so difficult. All too often I have seen people, when they are starting their investment journey, laying too much emphasis on the rate of return they expect to get from a particular investment. And in almost all the cases I have seen, they keep on waiting on the pretext of analysing the investment options and keep their funds in the savings account which, first of all, earns very low interest and, secondly, has a higher chance of being spent.

It's ironical to see that the same person looking for a higher return has parked his money in the tool with the lowest return. A higher rate of return is like the icing on the cake. But for that you need to have the cake in the first place. And where does this cake come from? It is your principal amount that you have put into some investment tools. So don't wait for the cherry. Get going with the base and cherry will come automatically.

Investing is putting your hard-earned money into an environment which you feel is safe and at the same time offers the opportunity for it to grow. If you follow the principles discussed here and avoid the common mistakes most people make, you'll watch your money grow to a kind of tipping point, where it can begin to generate enough in interest and dividends to provide the income you need for the rest of your life without touching the principal amount, that is, the base of the cake.

Now hopefully you have a better understanding of the popular investment tools. You just need to remember to establish your Emergency Fund Account by investing in FDs, then try to fill that PPF bucket and then start investing in index funds and ultimately graduate to investing in individual stocks and real estate. You should never invest in something which you don't understand completely and never invest in something if the risk robs your peace or your spouse's. Life is too short for you to keep awake.

Money is a wonderful servant. It is diligent and works harder than you do. It never gets sick, is never disabled and most importantly it never sleeps. Money works 24 hours a day, seven days a week and 365 days a year. Money gets its job done and it asks for only directions and a firm master. Be a firm master and your money will take your orders sincerely and help you become what you want to become—rich and prosperous.

Endnotes

1. The idea behind this story has been inspired from the story told by Warren Buffett, chairman of Berkshire Hathaway Inc. in the firm's 2005 Annual Report and discussed in the John Bogle's book *The Little Book of Common Sense Investing* in Bogle's version.
2. Active funds often distribute substantial short-term capital gains to their shareholders—which are taxed at higher ordinary income rates, not the lower long-term capital gains rate—investors in active funds face substantial tax burdens that index investors do not face.
3. You may find it comforting that in establishing a trust for his wife's estate, Warren Buffett directed that 90 per cent of its assets be invested in a low-cost S&P 500 Index fund.
4. Read this article: Jason Zweig, 'Did You Beat the Market?' *Money*, January 2000.
5. Alpha is a statistical measure which gauges the performance of an investment against a market index used as a benchmark. The excess returns of a fund relative to the return of a benchmark index is the fund's alpha.
6. http://www.thehindu.com/business/Economy/an-active-ride-the-passive-way/article18190978.ece
7. Economists and practitioners assign three levels of efficiency to a market. This is what is usually called 'Efficient Market Hypothesis'. While explaining the technical details is beyond the scope of this book, readers are encouraged to read about it. https://www.investopedia.com/terms/e/efficientmarkethypothesis.asp
8. As on 31 March 2017 as reported by NSE on its website.
9. This story of Sir John Templeton has been shared by Tony Robbins in his book *Money: Master the Game.*
10. This particular example of 'Lion in the zoo' has been explained in the book *Financial Peace* by Dave Ramsey.
11. This list of controls have been taken from the book *The Intelligent Investor* by Benjamin Graham.

PROTECT THE TREE AND RELISH THE FRUITS

Chapter 14

Protect Your Family

It was the rainy season of the year and the farmers of Sonpur town were taking extra precaution to protect their harvested crops. However, there was continuous downpour for almost a week and very soon the barrage which the farmers had built on the river broke.

When the people woke up in the morning, they found that all the crops in the fields close to the river banks were completely destroyed by the flood. However, those in the fields either far from the river bank or on a higher plane close to the mountains were intact.

This loss of crops made a huge impact on the economy of the town for a short term. First, the farmers who had lost their crops were left with nothing and were forced to go empty stomach for many days until they got some job. Second, the shortage of crops in the market resulted in prices shooting up. While the farmers whose crops were saved made a killing, a large population of the town found it difficult to buy food for their families.

As time progressed, life returned to normal in Sonpur. People had almost forgotten the incident of flood when suddenly on a stormy day a mild fire broke out uphill in the forest. As the wind blew, the fire of the mountains spread to the town and all the crops lying adjacent to the foothills turned into ashes. This time it was the farmers who had their field near the hill that lost their crops while the farmers near the rivers had their crops intact.

Seeing these two back-to-back natural calamities, the town chief thought that there were certain calamities which could not be avoided. They were bound to happen. However, they did not know when they would happen. While they could try to protect themselves by creating a barrage on the river and building a small canal near the foothills, they did not know with how much force and power the next calamity would strike. There was one good thing about these natural calamities though. They did not affect all the people at the same time and in the same proportion. So there had to be some way in which they could protect all the people together.

The next day the town chief met Thakur, the head of the bank, and sought counsel from him as to how they could help people in times of natural calamities. Thakur, after giving a thought to this, said that since these natural calamities didn't affect all the people at the same time and in the same proportion, they could pool resources from all the people which could be re-distributed in times of calamities such as fire, floods, epidemics and famine. He told the town chief that he would introduce a product in the bank where the people would be asked to deposit a small amount of money every year and in case they were affected by some natural calamities like flood or loss of someone in their family, they would get a large amount of money which would compensate for the loss of their crops or their family members. Since everyone would be depositing this amount, so the small funds from the entire population of the town would become a large fund and since it would be distributed back to only a handful people (affected by the unforeseen tragedies), it would be manageable.

'Do you think it will work?' asked the chief.

'Sure, it will work. We will tell people that by depositing a small amount of money, they are basically insured. And no matter whether there is a flood or not and whether the bread earner of the family is alive and earning or he has left them, they will have food to eat. And since everyone likes security, they will take part in this. I am pretty sure that this new product we call "Insurance" will be a success. In fact, it's a very noble product as this helps redistribute the risk among the people,' said Thakur.

'Yes, it is something like people who have lost their crops or loved ones will be helped by those who still have their crops and earning members with them. And since people don't know when they will be the next victim, they will come and take part in this. I think it will work,' said the chief.

So for the next week, Thakur was busy doing the math and calculating how much deposit per year (read premium) he should ask the people for, so that they could insure their crops against natural calamities. And then Mohan was assigned the task to educate people about this new product and encourage them to take part in the programme.

Mohan, after touring the town and meeting every possible farmer and trader, came to the bank ten days later.

Thakur: So Mohan, it must have been very hectic for you trying to educate people about this insurance programme and convincing them about participating in this.

Mohan: True Sir. It was very hectic.

Thakur: So were you able to bring in people on board for this insurance programme?

Mohan: No Sir. None of the people showed interest in this. In fact, after a few days people started running away from me thinking I was trying to fool them. I tried hard to convince them of the benefits of insurance but they didn't lend their ears to me.

Thakur: Why?

Mohan: Their main concern was that they would get nothing if nothing happened to them. Since they would be depositing coins with the bank, they wanted something in return. Also, many said that since these natural calamities don't come every year, why should they be asked to deposit money every year?

Thakur: But this 'insurance' is not an 'investment' where they can expect something in return. It is insuring oneself—that if something happens, then the rest of the family should not suffer financially. Though people do come out for the bereaved families with help in a friendly and unorganised way, but with 'insurance' we can actually make it happen in an organised way and the risks and sufferings one faces would be redistributed among everyone.

Mohan: That's what I told them. But none of them listened. They said that if they keep on depositing money and nothing happens to them then their entire money would go waste. Additionally, not many people want to talk about the loss of crops or loved ones. So it is practically impossible to bring them on board for this insurance.

Thakur: I guess they have a valid point. They should get something even if nothing happens to them. We can bundle investment with insurance and sell it to people easily. And, as with our other products, we will have a chance to make money. It's time to use their weakness for our own profit.

Mohan: But how can we do so?

Thakur: See, we will ask them to deposit money with us and tell them that if something unfortunate happens to them, we will pay them a fixed amount of money and if nothing happens, then too, we will pay them some amount of money. And if someone is getting money in both the circumstances then nobody would refuse to purchase such a product.

Mohan: But where do we make money?

Thakur: It is by charging a higher deposit (premium) from them and giving them a poor return in case nothing unfortunate happens to them. The difference in the amount would go into our pocket.

Mohan: And what happens when something unfortunate happens to them?

Thakur: In that case too, we will pay them less than what we would have had they gone only for pure insurance. Again the difference in the amount would go into our pocket. You know what is the best part?

Mohan: What?

Thakur: The best part is that while we will be collecting premium for both the insurance as well as the investment part of this product, we will be paying out only one part of it. If something happens to a policyholder, we will pay only the insurance part and keep the premium earned on the investment part and if nothing happens, then we will pay only the investment part and keep the entire premium for the insurance part in our pocket.

Mohan: Sounds interesting to me. Will they buy this investment-cum-insurance product and make us rich?

Thakur: They will buy this. If they want return on their money we will surely give it to them, but we will do it only when we have eaten a bigger pie of the return.

Mohan: Looks like I need to change my pamphlet and rush to the people with our new product.

Welcome to the World of ULIPs

Insurance as a product was introduced so that people could pool their funds and then redistribute them in times of unfortunate events to the victims. But as people didn't like to see their money going waste if nothing happened to them, they started demanding a return on their money and it was at this time that the banks and insurance companies saw an opportunity to make money. And that is what they have been doing by selling clever products to the people and making money for themselves.

It is not the bank or the product which is bad. It is the ignorance of the people which makes them lose their money. Banks see an opportunity to make money and just exploit the opportunity by selling you investment-cum-insurance (ULIP) products to you.

While banks and insurance companies do have pure insurance products in their portfolio, I have never seen them market these pure insurance policies and educate people about their benefits. However, I do get multiple calls from them telling me the double benefits and tax incentives that their favourite child (read ULIPs) would provide to me—or to them, I think sometimes.

So what exactly is a ULIP and why do banks and insurance companies love to sell them?

A Unit Linked Insurance Plan, popularly known as ULIP is a product offered by the insurance companies and banks that, unlike a pure insurance policy, gives investors both insurance and investment under a single integrated plan.

From the definition itself, it sounds so exciting that people don't read the fine print and purchase it instantly. A ULIP is a horrible financial product which plays with the emotions of the people and makes banks and insurance companies rich. The premium these ULIPs charge for the sum assured is way too high than the premium charged by pure insurance (Term Insurance). But you may say that they also provide return on money invested even if nothing happens to you. Wrong! They do not provide the return that you would get even if you had invested in something as simple as FDs.

Now assume Mr Ashish buys a ULIP with a sum assured of ₹1 crore (insurance part) and some return (investment part)—we don't know for sure what would be the actual return as it would be market linked and would depend on how long the investor has paid for it—and pays premium on it every year. Remember, the premium that Ashish is paying for this ULIP of ₹1 crore sum-assured is much higher than the one where there is no investment part since it includes a premium for the return part also in case nothing happens to the policyholder. Now suppose something happens to Ashish. What does Mrs Ashish and her children get? ₹1 crore. But what about the investment part of the premium that had been paying for so long? That cash value—the return for which Ashish was paying a higher premium goes to the insurance company.

Now suppose nothing unfortunate happens to Ashish. So at the end of the policy, how much does he get? He gets the investment part of his money which in reality is a very poor return on the total money invested. And what about ₹1 crore of the sum assured for which Ashish had been paying a higher premium? It stays with the insurance company.

Sounds a great business model! Want to open an insurance company which will sell ULIPs? Go ahead and sell them. But yes, never buy them.

And why do banks love to sell them? It is because they make a lot of money by selling them. I hope I don't need to give any more numbers to convince you how banks and insurance companies make money by selling those ULIPs.

Insurance is Not an Investment

The reason I wrote a separate chapter on insurance and didn't include it as part of the 'Investments' is because *Insurance is not an Investment* and you should never purchase an insurance which gives you a return on your money.

I have seen many people purchasing an insurance policy just because it was giving them dual benefit—a protection if something happens and a return if nothing happens. The general masses do not see insurance as a protection instrument, which it actually is. Rather their psychology is that if they give something then they should get something in return, no matter what. And that is how the banks and insurance companies play their game and make money.

In reality, combining investment with insurance doesn't serve either purpose effectively because you neither get adequate protection, nor high returns. So, you end up with insurance which doesn't really protect you and lose out on the opportunity cost because you could have earned more by investing the amount in a better instrument. Like I said earlier, even an FD would fetch you better returns than these insurance policies.

Now if you have invested in such products, you need to re-evaluate your options. The benefit of getting your money back, if nothing untoward happens, is actually a loss to you as, from the consumer's point of view, all these insurance companies are very bad money managers. Their costs are very high and the returns very poor. They were established with the sole purpose of insuring people and not to make their money grow. Investment and making the wealth grow is the job of the asset management companies (mutual funds) and not of insurance companies. If I want to make my money grow, I would rather invest my money in a low cost index fund. And if I want to take insurance and protect my family, I would go to an insurance company with a good claim settlement ratio.

When you go for an insurance policy, you should never go in for policies like money-back policies, endowment policies, guaranteed return policies, etc. because the only thing they will guarantee is poor investment performance with high fees and commissions.

Be alert and cautious about any life insurance that has a built-in savings programme. I think all the banks and insurance companies should put a board outside their offices, 'Beware, we sell ULIPs inside.'

Insurance is Not a Tax Saving Tool

Another marketing gimmick used by the banks and insurance companies is that investments in ULIPs can help you claim tax benefit up to a maximum of ₹1.50 lakh under Sec 80C. And this they use so enthusiastically that they are actually able to sell ULIPs to a person who has invested in PPF and taken a home loan. Little does the person know that he can't claim a tax benefit because the ₹1.50 lakh bucket of Sec 80C has already been filled with EPF, PPF and the principal repayment of the home loan.

Insurance is meant to insure you and your family against a calamity. It is neither an investment tool nor a tax-saving tool. Never purchase an insurance policy to save tax. Purchase it with the sole purpose of protecting yourself and your family.

The Answer is Term Insurance

Well, if not with ULIPs, how do we protect our families? The answer is term insurance which is the pure insurance and you should purchase it only when you are going for life insurance. There is no savings programme attached to it and that's what makes it simple and cheap. It just provides the family of the policyholder with a corpus that can replace his income in his absence. And it does nothing more than that. The purpose of the insurance is to give you peace of mind so that you can focus on building your wealth through better investment tools and create a better and bright future for yourself and your family. Term insurance does exactly that.

Banks and insurance companies, while selling term insurance (which they don't like to sell much), usually highlight premium rates for thirty-year old buyers for twenty-year plans. It's a clever ploy because the premiums for this low-risk age band of thirty to fifty years are very low and people tend to purchase them. However, such a plan will end when the insurance needs are high. It is only when you cross fifty that your visits to doctors and hospitals increase. But with such plans, when you reach fifty the policy ends. So you pay premiums for twenty years and when you need the amount you don't get it because the policy has lapsed. Another win for the insurance company! So my advice to you is that don't take a fifteen to twenty year plan that will terminate when you are in your fifties. Buy a policy that will cover you till the age of sixty to sixty-five years.

Now many of you must have already purchased a ULIP and must be wondering what you should do with it. Well, as I have said earlier, knowledge dispels fear, anxiety and the possibility of you taking a rash decision. You made an unwise decision earlier not because you were unintelligent but because you didn't have proper information and knowledge. And now since you know where you made the mistake, it is time to rectify it.

Step One: Don't set much store by the premiums that you paid earlier. Those are probably sunk costs and you aren't getting them back. Step Two: Calculate how much premium you need to pay when you purchase a plain vanilla term insurance with the sum assured equal to the sum assured that your present policy would pay you in case something happens. Step Three: Compare the premium that you are paying now and the premium you would need to pay if you switch to a simple term insurance. Step Four: If the existing one is lower, stick with it. And if the new one is cheaper, switch.

In addition to buying a term insurance, get a medical insurance as well. While many of you must have received a medical insurance from your employers, it is better to keep an additional one in case you plan to retire from the company before time and start something of your own. And even when you plan to stick with your job, the medical insurance from your organisation will not be sufficient to cover you and your family as you grow old and the medical expenses rise. My advice to you is to dispose of your ULIPs and go for a term insurance and a medical insurance for your family so that all of you can live your life happily and peacefully.

Chapter 15

Become the Captain of Your Ship

Slowly and steadily, people of Sonpur were becoming aware of the mistakes they were making by availing of unnecessary loans. So some of them who were more disciplined and understood the follies of debt stopped borrowing money from the bank, while some others, who by now had understood how availing of a loan robbed them of their savings but could not say no to themselves, continued borrowing money. This overall reduction in borrowing money by the people hurt the earnings of the bank as the interest income that they earned on lending money declined.

Further, the disciplined folks who were able to say no to themselves and a bigger no to the society saw their savings increase. However, there was one problem with the increased savings. People did not know exactly where and how to invest their money so that it grew with time. Earlier they used to lend money to the bank and then the bank would return them the money with added interest income. But there were other opportunities available. Some people lent money to businesses, some purchased precious metals and other commodities and others invested in commercial crops. However, there was a lot of ignorance among a major chunk of the population when it came to investing their hard-earned money, since most never used to have surplus money to invest earlier as they were busy paying interest to the bank. Now that they had stopped paying that interest, they wondered what to do with their increased savings and surplus money.

Thakur, who was keeping an active watch on what people were doing with their money, called Mohan and asked if he had any solution to the decline in the bank's profit.

Thakur: Mohan, I was going through our financial report and I see there is a substantial decline in our earning.

Mohan: True Sir. People have started to learn the importance of being debt-free. Now they are not so easily influenced by our marketing gimmicks and the assumed prosperity that we projected to them. They are getting smarter.

Thakur: Yes. And that is the reason our bottom line is getting hit. We need to think of other avenues of making money.

Mohan: But our main source of earning is lending money and making people borrow from us. And if they stop, how do we make money?

Thakur: Did you notice that people now have surplus money and are having trouble in deciding where and how to invest it?

Mohan: Yes. I did notice that. Even the shopkeepers told me that people no longer purchase items on credit. And they are happy about this. They say that with this they don't have to worry about getting their money back as they get it at the time of selling their goods. Additionally, it has helped them save the commission they were earlier paying us when we reimbursed their bills. Now that people have stopped purchasing items on credit, they don't have anything to be reimbursed.

Thakur: Another reason for the decline in our profit. The shopkeepers have stopped paying us commission as they are getting their money directly from the customer. However, I see one way in which we can still make money.

Mohan: And what is that way?

Thakur: It is by asking people to give us their money for investment.

Mohan: Since it will be their money and we will only be helping them invest, then all the returns on those investments will go back to the people. Then how will we make money for ourselves?

Thakur: You are so naive Mohan. See, people think we are experts in handling money. So first of all we can very easily command a fee from the people for managing their money. Second, whenever we put their money into a particular instrument, we will get a commission from the people selling that instrument. So it will be a two-way income for us—one from people who invest with us and second from the people with whom we place people's money.

Mohan: But wouldn't people protest when we charge a fee from them?

Thakur: No. Why would they protest? We are offering them a service and for any service delivered we can definitely command a fee.

Mohan: So people will come to us with the expectation that we will manage their money and help it grow. But what happens when the return on the investment is not as per their expectation?

Thakur: We will blame it on the market.

Mohan: And what about our fees and commission? Will it be impacted on the return that the investment makes?

Thakur: That is the best part of it. We will charge them a fee as soon as they come to us and hand over their money. Similarly, we will earn commission from the investment instrument seller the moment we place the money with them. So our earning will actually be upfront and not dependent upon the return the investment makes. No matter whether the people make money on their investments or not, we will keep on making money.

Mohan: But what will happen when people learn to manage their money on their own? Will it not stop our income?

Thakur: We won't let that happen. We can always project ourselves as someone who is more knowledgeable and experienced in handling and investing money. Also, while we give them fish to eat, we will not teach them how to fish. We will keep on highlighting why managing money isn't everyone's cup of tea and project ourselves as the custodians or safekeepers of people's money who will help them become rich.

Mohan: And how will we keep them hooked on to us?

Thakur: We will give them a nice presentation and tell them through good-looking graphs and charts how we have meticulously planned out their investment. We will try to talk to them in simple words, but very wisely insert jargons during the conversation and by doing so we will be killing three birds with a single shot. First, people will think that we are here to take care of them as we will be spending time talking to them and trying to educate them about the investments. Second, they will be impressed with our technical expertise in handling money and third, while they think that we are trying to make them understand the investment process, in reality they would not have understood a penny as we will be talking in jargons and never give them the true and complete picture.

Mohan: And in doing so we will make them come to us month after month and year after year and keep on making money for ourselves.

Thakur: Now you are catching it.

Welcome to the World of Financial Planners, Advisors and Wealth Managers

In a world where information is money, smart people find any opportunity to make money whenever there is information asymmetry and ignorant people lose their money just because they are on the other side of the information asymmetry. As we discussed earlier, when it comes to money, ignorance is not always blissful. Ignorance can rob you of your money, your mental peace and your sleep and I have seen people losing money just because they chose to remain ignorant about personal finance.

What holds us back from getting started on the road to managing our money, investments and ultimately to financial freedom? It is our inertia. And for a lot of us it's the feeling that we have in our heads. We've been taught to think, 'This is too complex' or 'This is not my field'.

Frankly, the system is designed to be confusing so that you'll give control to the so-called 'professionals' who reap enormous fees by keeping you in the dark. And what makes the system appear so confusing? It's the jargon. However, once you get past the jargon, you'll realise that it's really simple and you really don't need the help of the 'professionals' until and unless you have a very big amount of money to manage.

Just like everyone with vested interests has been running propaganda and spreading myths among the masses, so have the new-age financial planners, advisors and wealth managers just to fill their pockets from multiple fees and commissions.

'You cannot handle your own money.'

'We are experts in managing people's money and will help you earn better returns than what you would earn on your own.'

'We understand your investment needs much better and we will help you invest your money in a better way.'

I guess the only one who understands me and my investment needs better than me is my wife and I listen to her and would recommend you all to do so. Take counsel from your better half and you will gain a different perspective which will put both of you on the same page.

Most of the people who go to financial advisors and planners think that they are going to a doctor, but they're not doctors. However, Ray Dalio, the founder of investment firm Bridgewater Associates, which is one of the world's largest hedge funds, has a different take on money managers and financial planners and advisors. He says the typical money managers are not going to help you win because they don't have the skills or resources to play in the big game either. 'If they did, you wouldn't have access to them.'

The fact is that there are people out in the market who are really geniuses in handling money and grow it at a rate which we would like our wealth manager to do. The only thing is that they live in a coterie and are accessible to people who can invest a minimum of a million dollars with them. But since a typical investor like you and me doesn't have that much capital to invest, we can't reach out to them and it is futile to discuss them and their investment strategy.

But all is not lost. Now that you have chosen to gain knowledge, you are no more ignorant about money and personal finance. And after reading this book you are more knowledgeable and have more wisdom about money and investments than the regular financial planners, advisors and wealth managers who come knocking on your door or send you a mail telling you about their so-called expertise.

There are multiple reasons why I am against people going to financial planners and advisors and investing money with them. The first and the most obvious reason is the fee they charge you when you invest money with them. This fee reduces the return on your investment and if you're not investing much money, even a small fee can cut into your returns significantly. Remember, if you don't have a huge portfolio and are just starting out then you may not be able to even afford a financial advisor. Learning as you go and allowing yourself to make some mistakes would be beneficial in the long run and this is what I recommend to everyone.

But you may say that they provide a service and hence command a fee. My question is: What kind of service do they provide? Do they help you with something you cannot do yourself? Do they have a consistent record of beating the market by picking the right funds for you? Do they really care for your betterment and have the best interest for you when they invest money for you? And, most importantly, can you really afford to remain ignorant about money and investments all throughout your life? If the answer to any of the above questions is no, then it is better for you to start managing and investing your money on your own.

All these financial advisors, planners and wealth managers don't invest money in stocks directly but put it into one mutual fund or the other. And since mutual funds already have a team of experts called stock analysts, whose only job is to allocate your fund to different stocks, then why do you need another so-called expert to allocate your money to different mutual funds? You are already paying a fee to mutual fund companies (both actively managed fund and passively managed fund charge fees; however passively managed fund charge lower fees) for managing your money, then why do you want to shell out more money for them just to pick the right mutual funds for you? And if you are intelligent enough and have decided to go with the index fund then you don't need any wealth manager or financial advisor for this. Just buy the index fund and keep quiet. And by doing this you save your fees at two levels. First you don't pay any fees to your wealth manager. Second, you bring down the fees by staying passive. And when you combine the two, you actually save a total return of around 3 per cent.

As John Bogle, founder of index mutual fund giant Vanguard says, when it comes to investing 'you get what you don't pay for.' A one-time engagement with an hourly financial planner can put you on the path to managing your own investments, which for passive investors essentially consists of picking one's asset allocation mix, arranging investments accordingly and staying the course with occasional rebalancing all by oneself.

The second reason why you should not go with financial advisors and planners (either offline or online) is that in most of the cases there is a conflict of interest between your advisor and you. Almost all the financial advisors and planners earn a commission from the mutual funds when they put your money with them and since they receive different commissions from different fund houses, in most of the cases they would recommend a fund to you from which they get the highest commission but which may not be the most suitable fund for you. You should understand that there is no such thing as completely unbiased advice when the person advising you is making money by way of commission.

In the investment world there is a word called fiduciary. The regulatory bodies such as Securities and Exchange Board of India (SEBI) on seeing the inherent conflict of interest in this financial advisory business have made it mandatory for all the investment advisors and planners to take a fiduciary oath which simply states that they will put their client's interest ahead of their own. Remember, it's just an oath and not legally enforceable. And I have seen too many oaths being broken when money and greed come into picture.

The third and the most important reason why you should not go to a financial advisor and planner is that you and your habits don't change when you allow someone else to manage money for you. You can't have someone else lose weight for you. Your dietician can't do it and neither can your gym instructor. If you want to be physically fit then you need to take the proper diet and you have to work out. If you want to win a 100 metre race then your coach can't do it for you. He can only guide and motivate you but you have to do the real running. Similarly, if you want to be financially fit, then you need to take control of your financials. You need to learn to manage your money on your own. Turning all your problems over to someone else will only treat the symptom and not cure the problem.

Become the Captain of Your Ship

When it is your ship, your journey and your destination, it is better to be your own captain. And that is why I recommend everyone to manage their money on their own. More than the fees and commission, it is about you, your habit, your behaviour and your knowledge and understanding about money and personal finance. I am not telling you that all financial planners and advisors are bad or evil people and you should stay away from them. I personally know some of the financial advisors who work in the best interest of their client and I can tell you they are really nice guys.

What I am trying to tell you is that you cannot and should not put the reins of your life in the hands of someone else. It is your life and you should be your own master. God did not give them—financial planners and advisors—the responsibility over your money. He gave that to you. Celebrities and athletes often lose their entire fortunes because they give up the responsibility of managing their own money. The money manager who loses your hard-earned investments won't live with the regret and pain that you will.

Remember, always manage your own money. But at the same time you should surround yourself with a team of people smarter than you. You can tell if they are smarter than you if they can explain complex issues in ways that you can understand. If a member of your team wants you to do something 'because I say so', get a new team member. You are not hiring a boss; you are gathering counsel.

And who are your team members? Well they are a good chartered accountant, a tax expert, an insurance pro and an investment pro among others. Meet them, consult with them, pay them their consulting fees, learn from them but when it comes to investing, use your own judgement and take the decision yourself. By doing so, you will be getting multiple benefits.

First, you will not be paying investment advisory fees. You would be paying consulting fees but it is much less than the 1 per cent fees they charge for the asset under management (AUM) and the return on your investment will increase.

Second, there is no conflict of interest here as the person guiding you on various investment options will not be getting any commission since you are not buying any investment product through him and the chances of your getting unbiased advice would be much higher. He will be teaching you and explaining to you the myriad worlds of investment, taxation and insurance and in return you will be paying him his teaching fees. It is very similar to you learning from them and writing the exam on your own. However, when you let someone else manage your money you ask them to take the exam on your behalf—not sound advice I would say.

Third, you will be wiser as you learn the intricacies and nitty-gritty of the investment world.

Fourth, you will be in control of yourself and taking steps to improve yourself.

And when selecting and working with your wealth team, it is vital to bring only those members on board who have the heart of a teacher, not the heart of a salesman or the heart of an 'expert'. The salesman is always chasing a commission and thinking short term, and the 'expert' can't help you become an expert because by doing so he fears he would lose his edge over you. So go out and seek a teacher. Also, when taking advice, evaluate if the person giving the advice will profit from the advice. If your insurance pro comes up with greater insurance ideas every week, you may have a problem. That is not to say everyone who makes a commission off you is out to get you. There are plenty of commission-only financial people who have extreme levels of integrity. Just be aware of possible conflicts of interest and then you may be able to take a better call for yourself.

It is not enough to be an expert in your chosen area of your profession. You can be an excellent doctor but if you choose to remain ignorant about money and personal finance, you may end up broke. Similarly, you may have multiple patents in your name and yet be broke and you may be the best professor in your domain and still be struggling with your money. To take advice from someone who is more knowledgeable than you is a good and welcome step towards learning and growing but to let someone manage your money is bad and injurious to your financial health in the long run. And that is why, I often tell people to have dual skills—one which helps you earn money and the second which helps you manage and make your money grow.

And before I conclude this chapter, I would like to share a part of the column which Scott Burns, an MIT graduate, renowned columnist and author, who has covered personal finance and investments for over forty years, once wrote.

> I came of age in Boston. There are a lot of smart people there. If you doubt it, just ask them.

I could easily populate this column with the brilliant money manager of the moment. I also enjoy listening to smart, articulate people.

But forty years of investing have taught me that rented brains seldom help us build our nest eggs. Rented brains feel a deep spiritual need to build 20,000-square-foot log cabins in Jackson Hole with the return on our money.

That's why some readers will think I am Johnny One Note, always writing about investment expenses rather than the hot fund, product or stock of the moment.

But indexing and keeping things simple is the way for you and me to succeed. The other ways are how Wall Street succeeds. Big *difference*.[1]

Endnotes

1. The Future of Old, http://www.uexpress.com/scott-burns/2005/11/6/the-future-of-old

It's Just the Beginning

Thank you for taking out time to read this book and I hope you enjoyed it. Now that you have gained knowledge, wisdom and information on financial markets, institutions, players and the system, you are much more financially literate than most of your bankers, brokers and advisors. But being financially literate and being rich are like the two banks of a river and to reach to the other side you need to pick up a boat, set the sail and row against the current. However, there are many obstacles, both real and unreal, people face in their journey. And it is only when we overcome those obstacles and go past them that we can get what we have always desired—wealth and prosperity.

In this concluding chapter we will discuss some of them so that you are not only financially literate but are also able to create a path for yourself towards your journey of financial freedom.

Overcome Your Fear

Robert Kiyosaki in his bestselling book, *Rich Dad Poor Dad* says, 'I have never met anyone who really likes losing money. And in all my years, I have never met a rich person who has never lost money. But I have met a lot of poor people who have never lost a dime—investing, that is.'

We all are afraid of losing money and sometimes this fear grips us so much that we never say 'Hello' to the equity market. The truth is that the fear of losing money is real. Everyone has it. Even the rich people are afraid to lose the money they have accumulated. But fear is not the problem. It's how you handle fear. It's how you handle losing the money that you invested. It's how you handle failure that makes the difference in one's life. The primary difference between a rich person and a poor person is how they manage that fear. Brian Tracy once said, 'The fear of failure is the greatest single obstacle to success in adult life.' Note that it is not failure itself. Failure makes you stronger and more resilient and determined. It is the fear of failure or the anticipation of failure that can paralyse your thoughts and activities and hold you back from even trying to do the things that you need to do to be a big success.

A young journalist once asked Thomas J Watson Sr, the founder of IBM, how he could be more successful faster. Watson replied with these wonderful words: 'If you want to be successful faster, you must double your rate of failure. Success lies on the far side of failure.'

Self-made millionaires are not gamblers, but they are always willing to take calculated risks in the direction of their goals to achieve greater rewards. The joy of winning far outweighs the fear of losing for them. In fact, your attitude towards risk taking is probably the most important indicator of your readiness to become wealthy. Whenever you are faced with a risky situation, ask yourself this question, 'What is the worst possible thing that could happen if I go ahead?' Then, as J Paul Getty, the self-made oil billionaire, said, 'You should make sure that, whatever it is, it doesn't happen.'

Everyone is afraid of loss and poverty. Everyone is afraid of making a mistake and facing a setback. But self-made millionaires are those who consciously face this fear and take action anyway. Ralph Waldo Emerson wrote, 'Make a habit throughout your life of doing the things you fear. If you do the thing you fear, the death of fear is certain.'

When you act boldly, unseen forces will come to your aid. And every act of courage increases your courage and capacity for courage in the future. Whenever you take action in a forward direction with no guarantees of success, your fears diminish and your courage and self-confidence increase. You eventually reach the point where you are not afraid of anything.[1]

In my own life, I have noticed that winning usually follows losing. Before I finally learned to ride a bicycle, I first fell down many times. Before I learnt swimming, I almost drowned many times, in the swimming pool of course. And before making some real money, I have lost money. I have never seen an athlete who hasn't lost a game. I have never met people who have fallen in love who have never had their heart broken. And I have never met someone rich who has never lost money.

So for most people the reason they don't win financially is because the pain of losing money is far greater than the joy of being rich. People are so afraid of losing that they lose eventually.

Remember, if you want to become rich then you need to take up another job in addition to what you are doing presently as your main profession. And what is this second job? This second job for you is to commit yourself to becoming a self-made millionaire. This second job requires you to set specific goals for yourself, write them down and work towards them every day. And you must continue to remind yourself, in the face of all the problems and difficulties that you will experience in your journey, that 'failure is not an option', This is the attitude that, more than anything else, will guarantee your long-term success.

Invest in Yourself

The only real asset that anyone is born with and which stays with him all throughout his life is his brain. Strangely, it is one asset class which is least invested and remains idle—unused and untapped.

So what exactly is meant by investing in yourself? It only means that you need to keep on working on yourself by becoming bigger, better and more knowledgeable than what you were yesterday. And once you become bigger, better and more knowledgeable, you increase your capability to achieve more than what you were capable of achieving yesterday. As the old saying goes, 'To have more than what you've got, you need to become more than you are.'

What you become is far more important than what you get. Because once you become what you desire to be, then you can very easily attract what you deserve to have. Most of what you have today is what you have attracted to your life by becoming the person you are today. Income rarely exceeds personal development. Sometimes income takes a lucky jump but, unless you learn to handle the responsibilities that come with it, it will usually shrink back to the amount you can handle. It's hard to keep that which has not been obtained through learning and personal development.

At one of his Berkshire Hathaway's annual meetings, Warren Buffett said: 'The most important investment you can make is in yourself. Very few people get anything like their potential horsepower translated into the actual horsepower of their output in life. Potential exceeds realisation for many people. The best asset is your own self. You can become to an enormous degree the person you want to be.'

So how do we become more than what we are today? How do we invest in ourselves? And how do we achieve what we deserve to get? It is when we start doing all of these things.

- Read books and biographies: Books are a great treasure of knowledge and wisdom. They also give one an opportunity to learn and understand how all the great and successful people think. The only way one can access the vast mental power of the likes of Warren Buffett, John Bogle or Peter Lynch is to be humble enough to read them or listen to what they have to say.

  The reason most people lose money in their investments is that they simply buy the investment products rather than first learning about investments.
- Find someone who has done what you want to do: No matter what level we reach and what we become in terms of wealth, there will most likely always be someone who will be doing better. The realisation of this fact has multiple benefits. First, it will take out the arrogance from you and make you humble—a key trait if you truly want to become rich and successful and second, it will open doors for you to learn something new. Now that you know that there is a better player out there, try and take them to lunch or dinner and, while you order a starter for them, let them speak. Ask them how they did it, whom they read about and whom they meet and ask for directions in their journey.

  And this exercise again has multiple benefits: First of all they will be very happy to have a free dinner. Second, they will feel good and the chances of you two becoming friends are high. Third, they will happily tell you about their journey. And, most importantly, they may often tell you a very simple thing you may have missed noticing earlier just because nobody told you before.

One special quality of all the rich and successful people is that they know they don't know everything and that is the reason they are in the habit of learning continuously—seeking knowledge and wisdom. They are students throughout their life and that is how they become so rich and successful. Ray Dalio, the founder of one of the world's largest hedge funds says, 'What has been very successful for me through my whole life is to not be arrogant about knowing, but to embrace the fact that I have weaknesses; that I don't know a lot about this, that and the other thing. The more you learn, the more you realise you don't know.'

So what will happen when you realise that you don't know many things? You will start taking out time to learn about them. You will become curious and start seeking knowledge and wisdom. And that is the step you would take to start investing in yourself to make yourself bigger and better.

Take Action

Now that you have read this book, you have already taken a big step towards creating and accumulating wealth. In my experience, however, reading alone will not make the difference you are looking for. Reading is a start, but if you want to succeed in the real world, it's going to be your actions that count.

It is often said that busy people are often the laziest ones. Whenever I have talked to people to get their financial lives in order, I have often met with some kind of resistance from them. They say they are too busy in their work schedule and in getting the next hike that they don't have time to take care of their wealth. And these are also the same people who are too busy to take care of their health unless their visit to the nearby clinic becomes a routine. The cause is the same. They're busy and they stay busy as a way of avoiding something they do not want to face.

Remember what we had discussed in the chapter on 'Goals'—that most people confuse activity with accomplishment. Focusing too much energy on something that will not help you much is a waste of your energy. However, deciding what is important and taking actions in that particular direction is the judicious use of your time and energy.

Now that you have learned what money and personal finance is and how debts, loans and credit cards rob you of your money and how, by leading a frugal lifestyle and by investing your money regularly, you can truly become what you deserve to be, it is time that you put those principles and knowledge into action. While reading on the importance of taking actions, I found this great poem[2] from the depression era. I liked it and found that it applies in today's world as well. Read it!

The Rooster and the Hen

Said the Little Red Rooster,
'Believe me, things are tough!
Seems the worms are getting scarcer
And I cannot find enough.
What's become of all those fat ones?
It's a mystery to me.
There were thousands through that rainy spell,
But now, where can they be?'

But the Old Black Hen who heard him
Didn't grumble or complain,
She had lived through lots of dry spells;
She had lived through floods of rain.
She picked a new and undug spot.
The ground was hard and firm.
'I must go to the worms,' she said
'The worms won't come to me.'

The Rooster vainly spent his day
Through habit, by the ways
Where fat round worms had passed in squads
Back in the rainy days.
When nightfall found him supperless,
He growled in accents rough,
'I'm hungry as a fowl can be,
Conditions sure are tough.'

But the Old Black Hen hopped to her perch
And dropped her eyes to sleep
And murmured in a drowsy tone,
'Young man, hear this and weep.
I'm full of worms and happy
For I've eaten like a pig.
The worms were there as always,
But, boy, I had to dig!'

Success is Predictable

Brian Tracy once said 'Success is predictable.' So true! Success is not a matter of luck or accident or being in the right place at the right time. Success is as predictable as the sun rising in the east and setting in the west. By practising the principles that you have just learned, you will move to the front of the line in life. You will have an incredible advantage over people who do not know or use the knowledge and principles discussed in the book. You will have an advantage that will give you the winning edge for the rest of your life.

If you do the things that other successful people do persistently, nothing in the world can stop you from becoming a big success yourself. There are no limitations to what you can do, have or be, except the limitations you place on yourself by your own thinking.

You are as good as or better than anyone you will ever meet. You are an outstanding human being. You have talents and abilities far greater than anything you have ever realised or used up to now. You have within you the potential to accomplish wonderful things in your life. Your greatest responsibilities are to dream big dreams, decide exactly what you want, make a plan to achieve it, practise the strategies, avoid the myths, take action every single day in the direction of your dreams and goals and resolve to never, never, never give up. When you take these actions, you put yourself on the side of the angels. You become unstoppable and your success becomes inevitable.

Endnotes

1. *The 21 Success Secrets of Self-Made Millionaires*, Brian Tracy (2000).
2. The Rooster and the Hen, http://plainoldkristi.blogspot.com/2008/08/rooster-and-hen.html